ParaPro Assessment **Preparation** 2023-2024

Study Guide with 300 Practice Questions and
Answers for the ETS Praxis Test
(Paraprofessional Exam Prep)

EMILY MORTON

25% OFF Online ParaPro Test Prep Course!

Dear customer,

We consider it an honor and a privilege that you chose our ParaPro Study Guide. As a way of showing our appreciation and to help us better serve you, we have partnered with Mometrix Test Preparation to offer **25% off their online ParaPro Test Prep Course**. Many online prep courses are needlessly expensive and don't deliver enough value. With their course, you get access to the best ParaPro prep material, and you only pay 3/4 of the price.

Mometrix has structured their online course to perfectly complement your printed study guide. The ParaPro Course contains **in-depth lessons** that cover all the most important topics, video reviews that explain difficult concepts, over **350 practice questions** to ensure you feel prepared, and more than **678 digital flashcards**, so you can study while you're on the go.

Online Medical-Surgical Nurse Prep Course

Topics Covered	Course Features
Reading • Persuasive Techniques, Arguments and Logical Errors, and More **Writing** • Parts of Speech. Agreement and Sentence Structure and More **Mathematics** • Numbers and Operations, Systems of Equations and More **Classroom Instruction** • Learning Environments, Disorders, and More	**ParaPro Study Guide** • Get content that complements our best-selling study guide. **Full-Length Practice Tests and Flashcards** • With over 350 practice questions and 678 digital flashcards, You can test yourself again and again **Mobile friendly** • If you need to study on the go, the course is easily accessible From your mobile device.

To receive this discount, visit their website at **https://bit.ly/paraprocourse** or simply scan this QR code with your smartphone. At the checkout page, enter the discount code: **HP25**

SCAN HERE

If you have any questions or concerns, please contact them at universityhelp@ mometrix.com

"Successful and unsuccessful people do not vary greatly in their abilities. They vary in their desires to reach their potential."

— **John Maxwell**

Contents

Part 2- Practice Tests — 137

Introduction

Do you have an upcoming ETS Praxis test and not know where to start? Look no further, I'm here to help!

No longer will you fear walking into your exam unprepared. No longer will you be wondering what to expect! No longer will you question if your skills are up to par!

Within these pages, you will find everything you need to practice and prepare for your exam so that you can pass it confidently!

What is a ParaPro examination, and why do you need to take it? Since 2002, it has been part of the "No Child Left Behind Act" of the United States. It is one of the three courses you can adopt to qualify as a Paraprofessional.

If you want to qualify as a teacher assistant in a school, especially a primary school or a paraeducator, you need to take this test. As a paraprofessional, your job will assist the teacher and help the students learn. You may also need to stay back after school hours to 'tutor' students who struggle in some areas of study.

A paraprofessional also aids students with special needs by providing guidance and assistance. Of all education systems, primary education is the most fundamental and crucial. Your job will add positive meaning to children's lives and it's very rewarding.

The test is for 2.5 hours, at which time you have to answer 90 questions, 30 each from reading, writing, and mathematics. It has six parts and includes the following:

- Reading Skills- 18 questions
- Application of reading skills- 12 questions
- Writing skills-18 questions
- Application of writing skills- 12 questions
- Mathematical skills- 18 questions
- Application of mathematical skills-12 questions

The questions are in a multiple-choice pattern (MCQ), and each section has an equal scoring weight.

How does a ParaPro differ from other tests of its kind? It tests knowledge and skill in specific subsets of education: school education and their application in daily classroom practices.

I have carefully crafted this book into two parts. The first part includes three study guides. Each study guide focuses on one specific knowledge type and skill you need to successfully complete your exam. The second part of the book is reserved for practice tests. I have developed three practice tests for you to use. Each one will test the skills from the study guides. Don't worry, I'll also provide you with the answers so you can double-check your responses. My goal throughout this process is multifold. I want every student to be as prepared as possible, and I want them to successfully pass their professional exam. I also hope to provide students with an appreciation for the kinds of skills and knowledge required of them in their chosen careers.

What Do You Need For This Study Guide?

To go through the study guide and prepare for your exam, you will need;

- Pens or pencils
- An eraser or white out (Depending on what you choose above)
- Extra pieces of paper
- A timepiece of some sort to time yourself for the practice exams (Optional)
- Patience and excitement about learning!

You may not have a calculator to do maths!

I am rooting for your success! Let's get started!

Part 1- Study Guides

How To Use The Study Guides

The following three study guides are to help you prepare for the ETS Praxis exam. Each study guide tackles one (1) skill and area of knowledge that is needed to successfully complete and pass the exam: Reading, Writing, and Mathematics.

These study guides do not themselves include test questions; however they will include hypothetical and mock questions to illustrate points.

Be sure to thoroughly read through each study guide as many times as you like. You can use them at the beginning, throughout, and after the completion of the practice tests, as well.

NOTE: During the formal exam you will have no access to study guides.

Chapter One: Reading Study Guide

Reading is a foundational skill that is found and used in every classroom. Knowing how to read and how to pull specific details out of the questions is a skill that is necessary in day-to-day life and for a successful completion of the exam. It is also the skill that provides the foundation for writing and mathematics. For this reason, we've chosen to explore reading first.

Main Ideas

The *main idea* is the essence of the text. It fixes the purpose of the text and the course of the paragraph. Main ideas can be clearly expressed or implied.

Identifying and Understanding

The main idea is the primary thought or most important piece of information that the writer shares with their audience. The main idea is meant to answer the following questions:

1. "What do they want me to know about this subject?"
2. "What are they trying to teach me?"

Usually, the main idea is pretty easy to identify, as it is included in a singular sentence and separated from all other secondary pieces of information.

To determine the main idea, try to look at the big picture of the details listed. The key is to find out the three most important clues. They are as follows:

- The topic of the paragraph.
- What the author identifies clearly about the topic?
- The sequential arrangement of thoughts expressed and the major common details.

For example:

"People kept time by other means before the clocks were invented. People used a water clock in ancient Egypt. In this device, water dripped from one clay pot to another slowly, one drop at a time. Egyptians measured time by assessing how long it took one pot to get empty and the other to fill. Another variety of clocks is the candle clock used in the Middle Ages. Marks on the side of the burned candle showed how much time had elapsed. Across India and other nations, a Sundial was a method to keep time following the sun's movement in the sky. Shadows across the sun's face showed the time."

What is the main idea here?

Clearly, the main idea is the opening statement: Before more modern clocks were invented, people kept time by other means.

When in the form of a paragraph, the main idea is usually stated as the topic sentence. In a longer piece of writing, such as an article or essay, the main idea is the thesis statement which can be multiple sentences or even an entire paragraph long.

The main idea does not always have to be stated so clearly, however. It can also be implied or stated indirectly. This is called an implied main idea. To find an implied main idea, you have to examine the paragraph or the paper as a whole and consider what the main idea could be.

Identifying the main idea is imperative to understand what you're reading. The main idea is what ties the paragraph, the essay, or the story together in a thematic sense. In other words, it's what makes the rest of the piece of writing make sense. Without a main idea, a piece of writing can be confusing, scattered, and hard to read.

How To Find The Main Idea?

To find the main idea, you can employ the following steps.

1) First, define the topic of the piece of writing.

Knowing the topic before you determine the main idea is important. This is because it can give you hints as to what the main idea is. To figure out the topic, you can ask yourself, "What is this piece of writing about?"

2) Next, ask yourself what the author is teaching you about the topic?

Remember those two questions we mentioned above? This is where you ask them. Once you know the topic, then you can try to figure out what the writer is trying to tell you about it. Are they trying to inform you of its dangers, its history, or something else? As you can guess, depending on the topic, some main ideas simply won't make sense.

3) Use these seven clues to help you find the main idea.

a. Read the first and last sentence of the paragraph; the introduction and conclusion of the essay. The first and last sentence - and introduction and conclusion - is where an author will introduce and summarise their main idea.

b. Find and pay attention to repetition. The main idea is the most important part of any piece of writing. As a result, it will be repeated many times over. The whole text will be methodically woven around the main idea.

c. Look for a sentence stating the main idea clearly. Depending on the piece of writing that you are reading, the main idea may be highlighted, be introduced as a main idea, or have other indications that it's stating the main idea directly.

d. Look for clues to find the implied main idea. This will require you to read through the entire piece of writing and pick out words and phrases that are repeated and themes that are carried through.

    e.   Test it. If you are unsure if what you have found is the main idea, you can always try to test it. You can test your main idea by trying to summarize the piece of writing. Does your main idea comprehensively summarize the information provided? If so, then you've found your main idea. If not, then you may want to look through the piece one more time. Try to identify the *aim* of the author. Is it to state information (facts) or opinions?

The topic sentence is the sentence that contains the main idea. It is usually the first sentence but may not always be so. You should also look for "reversal." They are certain words or phrases that usually denote that the author may question the original idea when used in a sentence.

If they appear as early as in the second sentence of the paragraph, it may be the main idea. The second sentence, in that case, is the 'topic sentence.' Examples include, still, on the contrary, nevertheless, but, however, even so, unfortunately, yet, when in fact, regardless, conversely, on the other hand.

The main idea must be a complete sentence and contain a subject, a verb, and state a clear idea.

Example 1: Main Idea Implied:

Walking is good exercise. A regular morning walk, even for three to four minutes, is relaxing. You can have a walk-partner to share your day. Walking alone can help you to rewind.

In this example, 'walking' is the central theme, not exercise. You arrive at it by asking yourself, "what is it all about?" The topic sentence can be walking is beneficial for mind and body.

Also, ask yourself what the author wants you to learn? Read the first and the last sentences. Are they congruent? Obviously, the author wants to state the benefit of walking. Once you identify the theme, test it. Does it resonate with the information provided in the sentences?

Example 2: Reverse Transition of the main idea:

Modern health services are the crux of the nation's health. Clearly, the health services, as we know them, are essential, but equally clearly, they are not enough. There is an urgent need to blend the ancient traditional ways with some of the discoveries of modern medicine to make for a truly healthy society.

In this example, modern health services are essential *but* not enough. This changes the core of the text. Maybe, in subsequent sentences, the author will develop a more exhaustive option, which they do. This is an example of a reverse transition of the main idea.

Supporting Ideas

As the name would suggest, supporting ideas help support or hold up the main idea. Authors seek the help of supporting ideas *to bulwark the main idea*. When you read a paragraph, many questions may come to your mind about the theme of the topic. Consider 'who' or 'what' the passage is talking about. Identify 'when' or the time factor that's given in the paragraph. 'Where' is the place the author is talking about? Find out if there is a 'why' or the reason specified. Does the information state any methods, theories, or 'how'?

The supporting ideas answer them. Hence, they may seem more specific than their main counterparts and are too narrow of an answer when asked: what is this passage about? They include illustrations, numbers, figures, anecdotes, descriptions, clarifications, comparison, analysis, and other information to add details. The idea is to highlight the emotions and give evidence to the main idea. It entirely depends on what it was calling for.

Supporting ideas can be of two types. Major and minor. The author of the text can make points directly related to the main idea that are major supporting details.

On the other hand, the minor details back the major supporting ideas.

Let us look at the next paragraph:

"One must do a detailed job search to locate meaningful work. There are three main ways to look for a job. In the current world scenario, which is technological, people usually start looking for jobs on the internet. Many websites give postings on jobs together with information on the job descriptions. Another way to seek a job is to ask friends or colleagues engaged in the relevant field. One can ask questions about the job to gain information and discuss prospects.

Last but not least is to enroll in an internship or a trainee position in the field of interest. This can also allow an individual to gain a meaningful job. One also gains vital job experience during an apprenticeship. Therefore, candidates can locate rewarding jobs by scanning the internet, talking to individuals related to their area of interest, or accepting an internship."

You can identify the *topic of discussion* here: 'Job Searching.'

What is the author saying *about* the topic? What does he wish you to know? When you ask yourself these questions, you have the correct answer. The author wants you to understand the *methods of looking for a rewarding job*. This is the main idea.

Building on these factors, you can arrive at both major and minor supporting ideas. There are three big factors: *searching the internet* for meaningful jobs, talking to relevant people in your areas of interest or *reference*, and doing an *apprenticeship*.

The minor supporting details highlight the major areas of support. Let us look at them:

- *The internet and websites*: Postings of jobs, job alerts, job descriptions, and contact information.
- *Talking to people in relevant fields*: You can ask for and get information and learn about job prospects.
- *Getting a trainee post in your area of interest*: You can learn on the job.

The italicized text on the left-hand side is the major supporting ideas, and on the right are minor details that qualify the major ones.

Locating and Understanding

There are 5 Ways in Which a Supporting Idea Can be Recognized

Providing facts or examples from history:

"Queen Victoria became Empress of India in May 1876. Benjamin Disraeli, the then British Prime Minister of the Conservative Party, considered the new title would effortlessly link the Crown to the dominion, tying it closer to the British nation. It would also showcase Britain as a dominant power in the world. India had been under Crown rule since 1858 and before this under the dominion of the East India Company, who took control in 1757."

In this paragraph, the author wants you to know how Britain gained eminence as a world power; he has collated evidence in favor of his topic.

Providing comparisons through different ideas:

"Brisk walking for thirty minutes is the best possible exercise. Running is better; however, if you run daily, you may injure the ligaments of your lower limbs. On the other hand, you can walk daily without any problems with your feet."

The topic here is about exercising daily and identifying the best practice.

Providing emotional release or appeals to the reader's emotional side:

"Green vegetables are the best food. They are natural, fresh, and crisp with an earthy smell. It is easy to cook them, and you can even eat them fresh. Make a delicious salsa with green vegetables and add a slice of lime."

The author wants you to enjoy your green vegetable platter.

Providing humorous or informative anecdotes.

This is an account of a lady embarrassed by her untimely sneezes.

"I went to the supermarket with my mother. And, that day, I sneezed so bad! I tried to withhold my sneezes, but their urgency soon overcame my efforts. I moved to an obscure corner, one behind an empty aisle, and let out my sneeze. I sneezed three times and quite loudly.

And then they came one after the other. People stared at me, and my mother mouthed, 'What are you doing?' I just waved a hand and continued sneezing. I am waiting for the day when I can sneeze at my will."

Providing a definition of keywords or key ideas:

"Motion in Physics is the *change in position* of an object with respect to its *surroundings* in a given *interval of time*. The motion of an object with some *mass* can be described in terms of the object's *distance* traveled, its *displacement* from the original position, its *speed* and *velocity*, the time taken to travel the distance, and its *acceleration*."

Providing lists, charts, graphs, and images

Let us consider a different type of motion.

"A Motion is a legal method of application in writing to cite a matter relevant to your case to the judge. The things that you must include in a Motion are:

- Notice of Motion
- Memorandum of points and authorities
- Declaration
- Proof of Personal Service, or Certificate of Service by mail."

Facts vs. Opinions

In order to truly understand what you are reading, you have to distinguish between facts and opinions. This distinction is important as it helps you understand where the information is coming from, the legitimacy of the information, and if the information can be changed.

But why is it important to differentiate facts from opinions? How is it relevant if you are to become a teacher assistant? It is an important skill of a teacher to present their students with facts, and it is a matter of skill to sieve facts from the wealth of information delivered every day.

Differentiating facts from opinions tests your ability to judge critically and analytically certain statements presented before you. In any text, facts and opinions can be intertwined, and separating one from another will help an individual retain the beneficial things while discarding the others.

This is a skill that's excellent for lifelong learning. Whether you are reading a newspaper, an article on the internet, an advertisement, or the pages of a history book, you save yourself from misinformation if you master the skill of isolating facts from opinions.

Distinguishing Between Fact and Opinion

- Facts

  A fact is a statement that shares information about a person, place, thing, or idea. However, a fact can be checked and proved or disproved. That is, a fact is something that can be right or wrong. Facts are often *scientifically discovered* or have been *tested* in some way to be true.

- Opinions

  An opinion also shares information about a person, place, thing, or idea. But an opinion does not share what is true or false about the idea; rather, it's how the writer feels about it or what they believe to be true about something.

  Opinions are based on the personal bias and viewpoint of the speaker. In this way, an opinion cannot be proven true or false. You may disagree with an opinion, but that does not make it untrue. Likewise, you may agree with an opinion, but it may not be the real fact. You have to judge and employ your logic to conclude.

  Since opinions can be disguised as facts, you must watch the author's aim and his intentional use of language. The author may simply want the story or the points to allow the reader to arrive at a plausible conclusion.

"If fewer cars are on the road, it should minimize air pollution. Besides, sound pollution will also reduce because there will be less traffic noise. Therefore, we should encourage means of public transport."

The above example is a clear-cut way to tell you the importance of mass transport over personal vehicles.

However, sometimes authors may choose roundabout ways to arrive at a conclusion. Emotional appeal can be both positive and negative. You have to decide the rationality of the texts lurking behind the emotions expressed. That will help you to arrive at a fitting conclusion.

"Who likes to look at the soupy sight from a highway crammed with vehicles of all proportions? Cars honk, and irate pedestrians show their annoyance. These are the daily features in the cities and suburbs. Parking for cars is another problem. Tell me, do you enjoy road hugs when you ride to your work every day? And, what about crossing those myriads of road humps? Where is the joy of driving a vehicle? Mass transportation is the only solution to all these problems."

Hence, to arrive at a conclusion, ask yourself, are there enough facts, and are the facts reliable sources of information? If it is an opinion, ask if the opinion is based on facts or is merely stating some assumptions.

Signal Words

Sometimes the language can be truly confusing. Again, to save skin, study the word-play used by the author. There are times when the language itself will tell you how to differentiate facts from opinions. When the author is uncertain about the facts and is presenting his opinions, he uses words like *guess, disagree, claim, perspective, feel, view, think, 'some people say that,' 'goes without saying,' 'generally accepted,' believe, suppose, seems, considered, 'it's my impression,' 'I would like to point out,'* etc.

While stating facts, people use more robust words or phrases like *confirm, discover, ac-*

cording to, demonstrated, reality, factuality, genuineness, authenticity, data, figures, particulars, statistics, particular, etc.

These words and phrases will help you to discern the nature of statements made. Authors do not always intentionally present opinions and will unconsciously drift from facts to fiction in their writing. It is because of this reason you must develop a keen sense of separating facts from fiction.

These words or phrases are aptly called *'signal words.'*

A signal word is used to note whether or not a statement is a fact or an opinion.

Some other signal words to identify an opinion include *most, best, nicest, greatest, worst, better than, I think, always, never, delicious, revolting, nasty, for or against, oppose, or support,* etc.

Look for the context in which the statement has been made. A proper assessment of the context can help you differentiate facts from opinions.

But, what is a context?

The context describes the scenario in which an incident has happened. Therefore, two incidents can be the same, but the inferences will be different if their contexts are different.

A simple example would be a rainy day is enjoyable when you don't need to go to work.

Similarly, for any given statement, idea, or proposition, the context of the situation will determine the result. Contexts help us to understand and assess a situation.

So, a teacher says, "She is my favorite student," Before you conclude that the teacher is opinionated, you must look at the context in which she made the statement. If the student was weak but strived well to perform in the examination, she praised her efforts so as to encourage her. Others should learn from the student's example. The teacher's *emphasis* was on the efforts students should make.

A child who tells his mother that he ate a truckload of candies is probably exaggerating, but it is safe to assume he *ate a lot*. The mother may ask a *clarifying question* to turn the opinion into a fact.

During your test, you will be required to differentiate facts from opinions in a short time. You will need to get intuitive about evaluating what fact is. The more you practice, the sharper you become.

Inferences

Suppose it is 8 pm, and your father isn't home. You assume he is working late. When you visit the local grocery shop, and there is no one at the counter, you assume that the salesperson is taking a break. In each of these examples, you are making an *inference*.

The inference is reaching a logical conclusion from the supporting pieces of evidence. You study the evidence, make your own observation or opinion, and add it up to infer. Therefore, the inference is based on observation, scrutiny, evidence, facts, and analysis. However, like a hypothesis, the inference is guesswork, but it is a logical one.

For example, if you often see your friend in T-shirts sporting the name of a baseball team, you would logically infer that your friend is a fan of that team.

The inference differs from the hypothesis in using observations, evidence, and facts for a conclusion. A hypothesis is a prediction about something yet to happen.

In literature, before you infer, you must have a clear concept of what exactly you should pay attention to. Your objective is to be in the author's position and understand their perspectives. What do they *intend* to tell you? The intended meaning is what the author is trying to say to us.

Why is it important for you to make inferences? In a text, the author may not tell us about everything. They would prefer us to read their text thoroughly and use our intelligence and reasoning to arrive at a conclusion. The author is actually communicating with *you* through their texts, and they want the active participation of the readers.

You get to learn critical reasoning abilities and analytical skills when you can grasp the intended meaning of a text. It becomes simpler for the author to share all their ideas with you and easier for you to assess the writing critically.

The author cannot use specific words to describe something; it would make his texts dry. Inferences add excitement to reading.

"Sarah's face lit up, and she hooped in joy" is a livelier expression than "Sarah was happy."

Analytical reading allows the student to derive pleasure from reading the text in classroom studies. By probing the texts, you can make your teaching moments more authentic, illuminate their minds, and sharpen their reading skills. Children will learn to love books.

Inferences in science and mathematics refer to findings made from the data available. They are more accurate than literature. You need evidence and statistics to arrive at a scientific or mathematical inference.

For example, data may show that men aged 45-55 years are more vulnerable to heart and blood vessel problems, but the problems start a decade earlier.

The inference would be that men aged 35-45 years deviate from healthy lifestyle practices.

The synonyms for inference are conclusion, deduction, and consequence.

Therefore, inference is a process or method of drawing a conclusion about a subject using the information provided. Another way of saying this is that inferences are a method of reading between the lines to come to a conclusion.

To do so, you have to find clues in the text, paired with your existing world experience, to help guide you to see this new conclusion. Another way of understanding inferences is that they are guesses about the text based on the evidence provided.

Two Types of Inferences

There are two types of inferences; inductive and deductive.

- Inductive

  With inductive inferences, you make an observation about something or read the text through the lines to locate a pattern and then create or expand this observation and your opinion into a general theory. You use *evidence, patterns, and observations* to make an inference. This type of inference-making is more flexible, and you do not have to prove or disprove something. Students in school are encouraged to learn inductive inference making.

  Example: The individual observes a group of swans: some are black or white. An inductive inference to be made from this would be that swans can be black or white.

- Deductive

  Deductive inferences differ from inductive ones as they begin with a general theory, then move to a specific example to confirm this larger theory.

  Example: Let's say the individual knows that swans can be black or white. A second individual comes up and says that they saw a swan but does not include what color the swan was. The first individual can deduce that they saw either a black or white swan.

Therefore, an inductive inference keeps inference at the end. The deductive inference starts with inference and then looks for evidence for or against it.

But you should not make inferences hastily. Sometimes, the observations can suggest something different. For instance, how often has it happened that we've nodded at a passer-by without getting a response. We usually surmise that the individual is rude. but they may also be preoccupied with some problem we know nothing about.

A statement that says, "Her face turned livid," usually means she is furious, but that is not what happened with this boy from Ditte Everywoman by Martin Anderson Nexo:

"Sören picked up a hayfork and made for the lad, who hid behind the threshing machine, livid with fear."

Drawing Logical Inferences

Logical inference is the process in which we pull conclusions that make sense from the evidence.

Logical inferences have two main parts; the premises and the conclusion. The premises provide the information given to us from the text. The conclusion is what is drawn or the statement made from the premises.

Example in text:

Suzy and Johnny want to go to the park. But Johnny says that he will only go to the park if it is sunny outside. Suzy looks outside and sees that it is sunny.

What logical inference can we get from this? That Johnny and Suzy will go to the park.

Premise 1: Suzy and Johnny want to go to the park

Premise 2: Johnny will only go to the park if it is sunny outside.

Premise 3: It is sunny outside

Therefore; Suzy and Johnny will go to the park.

Sometimes conclusions can be drawn simply from the information and premises given, and sometimes additional information is needed.

Example in text:

Suzy and Johnny want to go to the park. But Johnny says that he will only go to the park if it is sunny outside.

What logical inference can we get from this?

Premise 1: Suzy and Johnny want to go to the park

Premise 2: Johnny will only go to the park if it is sunny outside.

In this case, a logical conclusion cannot be made because we do not know what the weather is outside.

Making Inferences

Let us understand how we can make an appropriate inference.

Ensure the Inference Fits In

Instead of depending on your feelings and views, try to understand the author's point of view. For instance, if the author describes Gillian Flynn's novel in unflattering terms, do not infer that the author hates Flynn just because you happen to admire Flynn's writing.

A Two-Step Method

Read the text carefully. Next, try to understand what each of the sentences tells you about the topic. Then consider the combined meaning of all the sentences; what you derive as the answer is the implied meaning of the text.

Desist From making An Irrational Inference

Once you have made the inference about the central thought, check it against each sentence. If the idea agrees with all of them, your conclusion is correct. If, however, your inference clashes with one of them, you are possibly making a wrong inference.

If the read is difficult, make sure that you understand the language or the observations that guided you to make the inference. This is reading your text closely; it helps you to remember things better and make informed decisions.

Transitions

The use of transitions in a text may mean that the author wants to guide the reader. They use transitions to help readers understand the meaning of the text.

Look for words and phrases like *consequently, next, in summary,* etc., to form links between different sentences in the text.

However, you cannot expect the authors to use transitions to help you draw inferences. It is primarily up to you. Even if a sentence does not start with a transition, you must grasp how the sentences you are reading connect to the general idea of the text.

Sentence Openers

There is a good chance that sentence openers can be the source of hints to make inferences about the given text.

Key Allusions And Idioms

Information in Graphs

Not all information that you read comes from words or in the form of sentences. Instead, information can be given to you in the form of images like charts and graphs.

Understanding and Using Graphs

To be able to understand and derive meaning from graphs, you should know the different kinds and what type of information they present.

- Bar Graphs

  Bar Graphs are used to show proportion but when there is no 'whole' to be considered. Bar graphs are usually meant to show a number of things in comparison to something else. Specifically, it shows the difference between a dependent and independent variable.

Independent variable: something that is discrete and valuable on its own. Also can be seen as the category of the study like gender, age, job, species.

Dependent Variable: something that is counted in relation and changed based on something else. This is usually counted numerically.

In the example of a bar graph showing how many people went to the movies in the years 2020, 2021, and 2022, the independent variable would be the year, whereas the dependent variable would be the number of people who visited the movies.

The bar graph begins with a large letter 'L'; the vertical line is called the y axis and the horizontal line is called the x axis.

- Line Graphs and Scatter Plots

  Line graphs and scatter plots are set up much like bar graphs. But instead of having a bar, they simply consist of a dot where a specific Y variable meets up with an X variable.

  When these points are not connected, it is called a scatter plot.

  Lines can also be drawn to connect these plots to show a clearer relationship and trend; this is called a line graph.

- Pie Charts

  Pie charts are used to show proportions or percentages of a whole. For example, what percentage of a population has brown, blue, or green eyes; or what percentage of a paycheck is to go to savings, food, leisure funds, etc.

  Pie charts are circular and have different sized 'slices' that represent different percentages. For instance, 50% would take up half of the circle, while 25% would only take up a quarter, etc. They are also used for items that are mutually exclusive of each other. The slices cannot have overlap. For example, someone cannot have blue and brown eyes.

- Bubble Charts

Bubble charts are images that use a variety of different sizes or colors of bubbles. It is meant to show data that is connected to each other. The relationships are shown through the size and colors.

For instance, dates or concepts that are connected will be in the same color while the size of the bubble will show importance; in other words, a larger bubble means the information is more important.

There is usually a legend explaining what the colors, sizes, and use for the chart are.

- Diagrams

A diagram is a sort of chart that features an image. The image is then labeled to help point out the different parts of the image. For example, a diagram of a cell will have a magnified presentation of the cell with labels for the mitochondria, the nucleus, the endoplasm, etc.

There is usually a title at the top of the diagram describing what information the diagram is sharing.

- Venn Diagrams

A Venn diagram is a kind of chart that shows shared characteristics of certain things. The image shows two circles that overlap each other at their center. The portions of the circles that are overlapping show the shared characteristic, while the two individual parts of the circle show the differences.

For example, a Venn diagram could be used to show the letters of the alphabet that are consonants, that are vowels, and that are considered both. The left circle would represent consonants and would include all letters except A, E, I, O, U. Whereas, the right circle would represent vowels and include the letters A, E,

I, O, U. The center portion of the diagram would include the letter Y as it is the only letter that is considered both a vowel and a consonant.

Reading Strategies

There are select strategies that can be used by the reader to help discern different kinds of information from the passage.

Skimming

Skimming involves the reader focusing on the main idea of a passage. When you are skimming a piece, you are speaking out this main idea and are skipping any information that provides additional or supplemental details to the story. These supplemental details can include stories, data, or any kind of elaboration.

When skimming, focus on the introduction, the first and last sentences, and any bold or italicized words that appear within the text. If you are skimming a chapter and a textbook, add to this list the chapter summary.

Skimming is meant to go by quickly and to get you the general idea of the piece. It's best to make the most of the time you have available and only read information pertaining to the main idea itself.

Scanning

Scanning means that you were looking through the piece of writing for a specific kind of information. It employs the same sort of method as skimming - that is, you are only meant to read pertinent information - however, rather than only reading the information associated with the main idea, you are going to read and find the pertinent information associated with your topic of choice.

Think of a robot in a Sci-Fi movie that is scanning a room for a heat signature. The robot ignores anything that does not have the specific heat signature it's looking for. The same philosophy applies to scanning.

When scanning, try to look for keywords and phrases that are associated with your topic of choice.

Author's Intent

The author's intent is the "why" behind the writing. The intent is what motivates the writer to create the piece and what they hope to achieve by writing it. For example, are they looking to persuade the reader of their opinion, to inform the reader of something, or to provide entertainment for the reader?

While the specific intention and purpose can be different and varied from piece to piece, there are only three general intentions. They follow the acronym PIE.

- To persuade
- To inform
- To entertain

Opening and Closing Statements in Paragraphs

Looking at the opening and closing statements in the paragraph is a method for understanding the gist and main idea of the passage without actually reading it. The first sentence is usually an introductory sentence, whereas the closing statement is normally one that sums up the ideas expressed in the passage. Using them together, you should be able to discern what the main idea and theme of the passages are.

Chapter One Summary and Key Takeaways: Reading Study Guide

This study guide was devoted to helping you further develop your reading and comprehension skills. Let's look at some of the key points in summary here.

- Main Ideas

    o Main ideas answer the question, "What is this passage about?"

- Supporting Details

  o Supporting details add information about the main idea.
  o They are narrow and specific in their content.

- Facts vs. Opinions

  o Facts are what is true or false - and can be proven as such.
  o Opinions are based on the bias, belief system, or desire of the person.

- Inferences

  o Educated guesses based on the information provided by the passage.
  o Inductive inferences begin with an observation and follow with the creation of a generalized theory.
  o Deductive inferences begin with the understanding of a generalized theory, then confirm that theory using a specific instance or example.

- Information In Graphs

  o Bar Graphs
  o Scatter plots and Line Graphs
  o Pie Charts
  o Diagrams
  o Venn Diagrams

- Reading Strategies

  o Skimming is the art of finding information about the main idea throughout the piece without having to read every word.
  o Scanning is the art of seeking out information from a passage associated with a specific topic.

    - Scanning usually employs the method of skimming.

  o Author's intent touches on the motivation and purpose for writing the piece.

- P- Persuade
- I- Inform
- E- Entertain

o Opening and closing statements in a paragraph.

- A method of reading that helps the individual make an educated guess at the main ideas and content of the passage without actually reading it.

Now that we have covered your skills in reading and comprehension, it is now time to focus on writing.

Chapter Two: Writing Study Guide

You will need strong written and communication skills to pass your ETS Praxis Exam. Most of your answers, even in the section on mathematics, will require you to clearly and concisely communicate your responses. Be sure to pay attention to see where you can apply these skills in the two other sections.

Parts Of Speech

Nouns

A noun is a word that references a person, place, or thing. You cannot have a complete sentence without at least one noun.

- Examples of person nouns: Harry Potter, girl, mom, Ashley.
- Examples of place nouns: the park, New York City, Canada, the bathroom.
- Examples of thing nouns: ball, the Eiffel Tower, finger.

In addition to the different classifications of nouns, there are two kinds of nouns: proper and common.

Common Nouns: Common nouns do not reference a specific person, place, or thing. Instead, they reference a general version of it. As a result, common nouns are not capitalized unless they appear as the first word of the sentence.

Proper Nouns: Proper nouns reference a specific person, place, or thing. Proper nouns are always capitalized, even if they are found in the middle of the sentence.

Sentence #1: "I am going to the *park.*"

In this case, the park is a common noun as it references the general park.

Sentence #2: "I am going to *Central Park.*"

In this case, both Park and Central are capitalized. The sentence is referring to a specific park and its name.

Verbs

A verb is a word that describes an action; that is what the subject of the sentence is doing. You cannot have a complete sentence without a verb. A good way to recognize a verb in a sentence is that it directly follows the subject, or you can put the word 'to' in front of the simple verb and it makes sense. A verb is often called a 'doing' word because that's how it's frequently used in a sentence.

Examples of Verbs; Sing (to sing), walk (to walk), thought (To think), know (to know), ran (to run).

Verbs can be changed based on the content of the sentence: you need to establish if the sentence is in the present, in the past, or in the future.

Example: To run (present), I ran (past), I will run (future)

Verbs can also be divided into physical verbs, mental verbs, and state of being verbs. Physical verbs are actions to do with our body, whereas mental verbs are actions that we do with our mind or in different cognitive states. State of being verbs are those associated with our existence.

NOTE There are other kinds of verbs; however, these are the three that act as umbrellas to the others.*

Physical Verbs

- Run, call, cry, shout, dance.

Mental Verbs

- Think, consider, believe, wonder, recognize.

State of Being Verbs

- am, are, is, was, to be.

Adjectives

An adjective is a word that modifies or describes the noun. Adjectives add more information to the noun, helping to clarify what kind, which one, and who the thing belongs to.

Examples of adjectives include any color (blue, yellow, purple), any description of size (large, small, wide), or any description of state or demeanor (old, busy, stormy).

Generally, there are two ways in which adjectives are used in sentences: Right next to the noun or pronoun, or following a verb.

- Beside the Noun

  This is when the adjective is directly before or after the noun and describes it.

  Example: *New* shoes, *orange* cat, *big* house.

- After a Verb

This is when the adjective follows a verb: but still describes and modifies the noun. *If the adjectives describe the verb or action word then it makes it something else entirely.*

Example: It was a **red** and *juicy* apple.

* in this case, was is the verb*

Adverbs

An adverb is a word that modifies or describes the verb.

Adverbs usually end in 'ly' as regards their spelling, but they do not always have to.

Examples of adverbs; badly, very, too, unfortunately.

Adverbs answer the question 'in what manner' or 'how.'

For example, let's say we have the sentence, "the cat ran to the ball." We can ask the question, how did the cat run to the ball, and in what manner did the cat run to the ball? Adverbs help to add detail here. With the addition of some adverbs, the sentence can change in a variety of ways.

The cat **playfully** ran to the ball.

The cat **reluctantly** ran to the ball.

Adverbs can also modify and describe an adjective or another adverb. In some cases, an adverb can also describe an entire sentence.

- Adverbs Describing Adjectives

Adverbs are used to describe adjectives, while the adjective describes the noun.

Examples:

Samson is an *incredibly* handsome boy.

- Adverbs Describing the Sentence

  An adverb that modifies the sentence gives the entire sentence a specific tone.

  Example:

  Fortunately, we made it to school on time!

- Adverbs Describing Other Adverbs

  When adverbs are used to describe other adverbs, it's usually when multiple adverbs are being used in general.

  Example:

  Fred sings off-key *loudly.*

Prepositions

A preposition is a word that helps to describe when and where an event happened, or when and where an object is in relation to something else. Prepositions can also show ownership.

- When

  Prepositions that show us when include: before, after, on a date, at a time.

  Examples;

  Dinner will be *at* seven o'clock.

  The party will be *on* Tuesday.

  We will go for lunch *before* we go to see the movie.

- Where

  Prepositions that tell us where include: over, behind, besides, on, at.

  Examples;

  The cat is *on* the couch.

  The shoe is *under* the couch.

  I am *behind* the tree.

- Ownership

  Prepositions that show us ownership include: of, for.

  Examples;

  The gift is *for* Sam.

  The legs *of* the spider were long.

Conjunctions

A conjunction is a word that connects different sentences, clauses, or even words. They are used to help with repetitive sentences, help to eliminate clauses or phrases in writing, and to help with the creation of lists.

Some of the most common conjunctions include; and, but, or, so, because, since, unless, however, while, after, that.

There are different kinds of conjunctions.

- Coordinating Conjunctions

  Coordinating conjunctions are used to connect two or more grammatical elements that are equal or of the same kind. For example, a coordinating conjunction can connect two verbs, two adjectives, two independent clauses, etc.

Example:

Heather skipped *and* jumped through the obstacle course.

- Subordinating Conjunctions

This kind of conjunction is used when connecting a dependent clause with an independent clause. A dependent clause cannot stand on its own as a complete sentence. It needs a conjunction to be connected to an independent clause.

These conjunctions can come at the beginning of the sentence or in the middle.

Example:

Whenever it is sunny, we play outside.

We play outside, *whenever* it is sunny.

- Correlative Conjunctions

  These kinds of conjunctions are pairs of conjunctions that are used together.

  Example:

  Susie wants *either* a pink *or* a purple popsicle.

  I would *rather* watch a romantic movie *than* a scary movie.

Interjections

Interjections are specific words that are used to show strong feelings and emotions. They are usually single words that do not actually influence the grammar or the structure of the sentence in any way. In fact, many times, interjections are single words that are considered their own sentence since they begin with a capital letter and are followed with some sort of punctuation. They can also be used within the sentence itself.

Examples:

Ouch! Wow! Yuck!

Oh no, he's going to fall!

Spelling Rules

The following are some spelling rules that are found in the English language.

For each rule there will be a definition, followed by an example of the rule, followed by any sort of exceptions to this rule.

I Before E, Except...

- Definition

  The rule is that the letter 'i' should always come directly before the letter 'e' when spelling the word, except when the pairing falls after the letter 'c'.

- **Example:**

  I before E

  Achieve, believe, chief, piece, yield.

  Not after C

  Ceiling, conceit, perceive, receipt, receive.

- Exception to the rule

The exception to this rule is that it only applies when the 'ie' makes a double e 'ee' sound. When the word does not include this double e sound, then the 'i before e' rule does not apply.

For instance: neighbor, vein, weight, height, forfeit, beige, science.

Silent E

- Definition

  When there is a silent e in the spelling of a word, it's for a variety of reasons.

  a. It makes the other vowel say its own name.
  b. It highlights consonant sounds.
  c. It helps to distinguish between homophones.
  d. To give each syllable a vowel.
  e. Stops words from being ended with a U or a V.
  f. There is a historical use of the letter e.

- **Example:**

a. Made, bite, note, cute - without the e these words would be mad, bit, not, cut.
b. Ice, age, (the e makes the C and the G make a soft sound) / please, cheese (The e tells the S to make the sound a Z).
c. aw-awe, brows-browse, by-bye.
d. Able, apple, bubble, circle (without the letter e at the end, then only the first syllable would have a vowel).
e. Argue, blue, wave, drive (without the e the letters would end with a V or a U).
f. Come, done, give, some (in all their variations of the language, these words may have been ended with an f.

- Exception to the rule

  There are no necessary exceptions to this rule; however, there are different variations to the rule, as we mentioned above.

Keeping or Changing the Ending Y

- Definition

    When the word generally ends in a Y, and we want to add a suffix at the end of it, then we must change the Y to an I before we add the ending.

- **Example:**

    The most busy; busy + est = Busiest
    Past tense of Rely; Rely + ed = Relied
    Past tense of Try; Try + ed = Tried

- Exception to the rule

    There are no significant exceptions to this rule.

Double Consonants

- Definition

    A double consonant is simply when there are two consonants right beside each other in a word. Rarely are these double consonants pronounced themselves in the word, but they often change and dictate how the rest of the word is pronounced.

    There are words that are always spelled with a double consonant like 'written', 'bull', 'pull', and 'grass'. But, usually, double consonants are added to a word when including a suffix to the word.

    a. Adding a suffix to single syllable words; add consonant - vowel - consonant to end of the word. The last letter is the double consonant.

    b. Adding suffix to multiple syllable words when the second syllable is stressed; make the last consonant double and add suffix.

- **Example:**

  a. Big -> bigger (g-e-r), Step -> Stepped (p-e-d)

  b. Begin -> Beginning

- Exception to the rule

  a. does not work when the single syllable word ends with w, x, y, or z
  b. does not work when first syllable is stressed like in water, spirit, focus

Prefixes and Suffixes

- Definition

  Suffixes are a series of letters that are added to a root word to change the meaning or the tense of the word. Prefixes are letters or a series of letters that are added to the beginning of the root word to change its meaning or tense.

- **Example:**

  Suffixes; Joy**ous**, Tender**ness**, Run**s**

  Prefixes; **Micro**scope, **Tri**pod, **anti**-establishment

- Exception to the rule.

  There are no necessary exceptions to this rule, the prefix and suffix are simply dependent on what you want the meaning of the word to be.

Forming Plurals

- Definition

  There are a few different ways in which you can make words plural.

a. Regular nouns require an s

b. If the singular noun ends with -s, -ss, -sh, -ch, -x, or -z, then you need to add -es

c. If the noun ends with -f or -fe, then you will usually have to replace the end with -ve

d. If the noun ends in -y and the letter before the -y is a consonant, change the ending to -ies

e. If the noun ends in -o, add -es

f. If the noun ends in -us, the plural ending is usually -i

g. If the noun ends in -is, replace it with -es

h. If the noun ends in -on, replace it with -a

i. Some nouns don't change at all when they are made plural

- **Example:**

a. cat – cats, house – houses

b. bus – buses, lunch – lunches, tax – taxes

c. wife – wives, wolf – wolves

d. city – cities, puppy – puppies

e. potato – potatoes, tomato – tomatoes

f. cactus – cacti, focus – foci

g. analysis – analyses, ellipsis – ellipses

h. phenomenon – phenomena, criterion – criteria

i. sheep – sheep, series – series, deer –deer

- Exception to the rule
- You may have to add an extra consonant if you want to keep the pronunciation of a vowel the same (gas- gasses).
- Some words don't abide by their ending rules; roof does not become rooves, it becomes roofs.
- Photo does not become photoes, it becomes photos.

Correct Spelling of Commonly Misspelled Words

There are an incredible amount of words in the English language that have some tricky spelling to them. Here is a chart detailing some of the most commonly misspelled words, and some tips for how to spell them correctly.

Commonly misspelled Word	Spelling Tip to Help
accommodate	This word can have both two "c"s and two "m"s.
achieve	Remember "i" before "e" except after "c."
acquire	Remember there's a "c" before the "q."
across	Let "Ross" row across.
address	Just when you thought there's only one "d" living in this address, there's two right together!
advertize	The ADVERT was revIzEd.
advice	I "c" that you gave me advice.
among	A "monk" was among the worshipers.
apparent	The AP ate with his PARENT.
argument	Gumbo lost an "e" in an argument.
athlete	Don't delete the "l" in athlete.
awful	It's "aw" but not so cute!
balance	The BAd man used a LANCE.
basically	It's BASIC that I have an ALLY.
becoming	B "E" the light COMING into someone's world.
before	BEe was called to go to the FORE.
beginning	"N" married "ing" and started a new "beginning."
believe	Do not believe a lie.
benefit	BENE is very FIT.
breathe	Take an extra "e" when you breathe.
brilliant	The BRILLo pad was gIANT.

business	I took a BUS. No empty seat IN it. What a mESS!
calendar	Dara checked the calendar every day.
careful	You'd think you would CARE to feel so FUL, but there's an L missing just like dessert from your plate!
category	The CAT's Ear is GORY.
ceiling	Remember "i" before "e" except after "c."
cemetery	The cemetery made Eileen e's.
certain	He's CERebral, so don't TAINt it.
chief	Remember "i" before "e" except after "c."
citizen	Don't CITe It; practice ZEN.
coming	Coming is too quick for two "m's."
competition	COMe PET IT, ION.
convenience	Remember "i" before "e" except after "c."
decide	Clide, remove the "l" and spell decide.
definite	DEb had a FINITE spending limit.
deposit	DEb POSITed that we deposit the money.
describe	DEb hired a SCRIBE.
desperate	DES, PER your direction, rATEd it.
develop	Lop off the "e" in develop.
difference	We DIFFER about pENCE.
dilemma	Emma faced a dilemma.
disappear	It takes two "p"-s to disaPPear!
disappoint	To make a disappointing point, introduce the "p" in point to another "p" and marry them!

discipline	The DISC Is Perfectly in LINE.
does	The DOE Sang.
during	DU bought a RING.
easily	The bEASt Is loveLY.
eight	There's an eight in height.
either	Ed Is THERe.
embarrass	It's very difficult to EMBArrass Rightfully Reasonable And Serious Sarah.
environment	A new environment will iron me out.
equipped	He "quipped" that he was E- "QUIPPED" for the job.
exaggerate	Goofy Greg loved to exaggerate.
excellent	The EXact CELL is bENT.
except	My EX is Certain I'm inEPT.
exercise	I "EXER"t energy pre"CISE" ly when I exercise.
existence	I EXIST with mike pENCE.
expect	I met my EX in PE, what did you expeCT?
experience	I am an "EXPER"t, I.E. (that is), an artist of da "NCE"
experiment	PER my EX, I MENTored him.
explanation	She is my EX. She's was "PLAN"-nning to cause a ruckus "AT" my school Un"ION".
familiar	That liar looks familiar.
fascinating	It's "s" before "c" in fascinating.
finally	"Final" is one l, but "Finally" has two!
foreign	"Fore"mentioned, he said, her "reign" was a good one.

forty	There's no "u" in forty.
forward	"FOR" Jane, he said, she was a good mother to the king's "WARD."
friend	It's only the "r" that could make the difference between a "friend" and a "fiend"
fundamental	Fundamental is just FUN, DAMEN, and TAL.
generally	Generally, a general is your best ally.
government	The GOVERNor was deMENTed.
grammar	GRAM didn't want to MAR our grammar.
guarantee	The GUARd ANd the TEEn guaranteed it.
guidance	Guy changed his spelling to "Gui" and went to "dance."
happiness	To get happiness, all you need to do is take the "y" from "happy" and put an "i" in place of it. After that, add the ness, and there you have it!
heroes	HE ROped an E for hiS heroes.
humorous	He HUMs fOR the mOUSe.
identity	There is an "ID" in identity.
imitation	Don't imitate. There's only one "m" in imitation.
immediately	Mom ate immediately.
incidentally	The "incident" made him my "ally".
interesting	The "INTER"national ball was the b"EST" way of sh"OWING" her off.
interfere	The INTERn watered the FERn, I sEe.
interpretation	The INTERn PRETended that stATION was near.
interruption	Don't interrupt: Interruption has two "r's."
invitation	INVITe me to offer a rATIONale.

irrelevant	Don't make the second "r" in irrelevant irrelevant. And there's an "ant" at the end.
	An "ANT" sat at the end of "IRRELEVANT". She told me to not ignore the second R, ever!
irritable	Set the "Table", and don't forget that "Irritable" has two r's!
island	An island IS LAND surrounded by water.
jealous	JEAn's a LOUSe to be jealous.
knowledge	I KNOW you can reach the LEDGE.
laboratory	I had to LABOR at orATORY.
length	Put a "g" between the "n" and the "t" in length to make it longer.
lesson	Spend "LESS" "ON" useless things!
loneliness	It's a LONE LINE with an SS in sight at the end!
losing	I like to hear LO SINGers.
lying, laying	The truth is that lying has a "y" but no "ie."
miniature	MINI A has no staTURE.
minute	Minute is MINU and TE.
mysterious	MY STERIO is for US.
naturally	NATURe has an ALLY.
necessary	The CESS-pool is a "NECESSARY" reminder of the state of things.
neighbor	The horse NEIGHed at the BORing man.
neither	NEIl Is THERe.
noticeable	The notice is able to help.
occasion	It's a good time to recognize that an occasion has two "c's" and one "s."
occurred	He realized that the word "occurred" has two "c's" and two "r's."
official	Old Franny Frankesting Is Clever, Interesting, and Lovely.

often	OF mice and men there were TEN.
omission	Leave out the second "m," but definitely don't omit the second "s."
optimism	Let's hOP with TIM into the schISM.
ought	Ought is "bought" minus the "b."
parallel	Two "l's" form parallel lines in parallel.
particularly	PART Is in the CULt with ARLY.
peculiar	It's peculiar the PECU is a LIAR.
perceive	It's "i" before "e" except after "c."
perform	PER the directions they FORMed a line.
permanent	The PERM on the woMAN looks expensive, but it's worth a cENT.
persevere	PER the directions, he SEVEREd it.
personally	The PERSON was an ALLY.
persuade	PER the SUn, he had it mADE.
picture	At the appropriate aperTURE, the PICture was taken.
piece	Have a piece of the pie.
pleasant	He tried to PLEASe the ANT.
political	The POL Is noT ethICAL.
possess	Remember that the word "possess" has two double "s"s.
possible	The POSSe Is BLEssed.
practical	PRACTICe will make your practicAL perfect!
prefer	PREp the FERn.
prejudice	Don't PREJUDge; think twICE.
presence	The PRESident chose pENCE.
privilege	Privilege is PRIVI with just a LEG as well as an E added to the end.

probably	He handled the PROBlem ABLY.
professional	The PROFESSor said that professIONAL also has two "s"s.
promise	The PROM date was a surprISE.
proof	I have confirmation that the word "proof" has two "o"s.
psychology	"PSYCH!" it's not socio, but psychOLOGY!
quantity	The QUANT Is TinY.
quarter	The QUARTEt is Ready.
quiet	Please keep quiet about my diet.
quit	Quiet lost its "e" and became quit.
quite	Quit added an "e" and became quite.
realize	The REAl man materiaLIZEd.
receive	Remember "i" before "e" except after "c."
recognize	Can you give me a "RECO" so I don't aGONIZE over prospects.
recommend	I think you should put two "m"s in the word "recommend."
reference	REFER it to mike pENCE.
religious	RELIGate the task to the pIOUS man.
repetition	REPEaT IT In unisON.
restaurant	REST until you and your RANT with your AUnt begins.
rhythm	Rhythm Helps Your Two Hips Move.
ridiculous	RID the Island of CUrious LOUSes.
sacrifice	It's a "sac" at the o"rifice".
safety	Safely add "ty" to safe to go and get safety.

scissors	Sarah Cut Into Six Slabs of chocolate on Orders from Richie Sims.
secretary	It's a "SECRET"-ary!
separate	There's A RAT in separate.
shining	Marty hurt his SHIN choppING wood.
similar	SIMI valley has a lot of LARd.
sincerely	Pair SINCE and RELY to get sincerely.
soldier	For the sake of his country, Sam advised Larry to be a good soldier and DIE.
speech	Stretch it out: Speech should have two "e's."
stopping	STOP and hear the PING.
strength	She Trained Really Efficiently. Nice, Given The Heat.
studying	"Stop playing the STUD and STUDY!" "I'm Study-ing!"
succeed	Two e's and two c's and nothing can stop you from succee-ding!
successful	To be successful, you need to put two "c's" and two "s's" together in SUCCESSFUL.
surely	Sure, just add "ly" to get surely.
surprise	The SURPlus caused inventory to RISE.
temperature	He has such a "TEMPER," she thought. So imm"ATURE"!
temporary	The TEMP Or Rick Ate Real Yogurt.
through	The "HR" manager took a "TOUGH" stance to get "THROUGH" the interviews.
toward	I TOW an ARDvark.
tries	It's like TIRES, but "I" and "R" switched places.

truly	Tom Really Understands Libby's Yeti.
twelfth	The TWin ELF THought about it.
until	You'd think the room needs more "TIL"es UNTIL it is done.
unusual	UNUSed, Uni Asked Larry for a loan.
using	Drop the "E" from "USE", and add ING instead!
usually	USU was his ALLY.
village	It takes two "l's" to spell village.
weird	Moving the "e" turns wired into weird.
welcome	WE Love COmmunists from MEndecino.
Whether, weather	I don't care WHETHER you like snow, the cold is my favorite WEATHER.
writing	Drop the "E" from "WRITE" and add "ING" instead!

Clauses

Generally, a clause is a grouping of words that includes a subject and a verb, and is part of a sentence. There are a number of different kinds of clauses.

Independent and Dependent Clauses

Independent and dependent is the most basic distinction between kinds of clauses, and it comes from the first word of the clause. It is also a clause that cannot stand on its own as a full and complete sentence.

A dependent clause begins with a subordinator like 'when', 'if', or 'which'.

    a. When we start the game,
    b. If we finish the project,

    c. That was my grandmother's,

An independent clause is one that can stand on its own as a sentence and it begins with any word other than a subordinator.

    1) Let's go to the store.
    2) I will give him the homework from today.
    3) The television is not working.

Every complete sentence needs at least one independent clause. A dependent clause simply adds more information without having to create an entirely new sentence.

Adverb Clauses

An Adverb clause is a dependent clause or group of words that act as an adverb and describe the verb in the sentence. They add information to the when, why, how, and where of the action in the sentence.

An adverb clause <u>has to</u> include a subject, a verb, and a subordinating conjunction. These clauses can be at the beginning, in the middle, or at the end of the sentence.

Example:

My mom, ***when she is stressed***, will eat a lot of junk food.

<u>We realized,</u> ***only after we submitted the exam***, that we had gotten the answer wrong.

Whether we like it or not<u>, we </u>have to start budgeting.

You <u>have to</u> keep working, ***until you finish the project.***

Adjective Clauses

An adjective clause is a kind of dependent clause - or a group of words that are not quite a sentence - that shows which or what kind of noun is in the sentence. It modifies the noun.

They usually begin with relative pronouns like 'which', 'that', or 'whom', but sometimes they can be implied as well.

Example:

That is the car ***that we are going to drive.*** *The car is the noun that is being described*

This doll, **which used to be my grandma's,** is my favorite. *The noun is the doll*

Have you seen the keys ***I lost?***

Simple vs. Complex Sentences

- A simple sentence is one that has a single independent clause. There is usually a single punctuation note.

  Example:

  a) I read a book.
  b) The dog runs after the ball.

- A complex sentence is one that combines one independent clause and one dependent clause together. It doesn't matter which kind of clause comes first.

  Example:

  a) Although we left on time, we were late to the party.
     Dependent clause, Independent clause

  b) Jake eats his carrots, even though he doesn't like them.
     Independent clause, Dependent clause

Grammar

Grammar is the system of rules that we have to follow when we write. It is what helps our writing make sense. There are a multitude of laws that underscore the system of grammar. We have collected here a list of seven (7) of the more useful, important, or mistaken ones.

Recognizing Simple Subjects and Simple Predicates

Nearly every sentence can be divided into two parts; the subject and the predicate.

The subject is the group of words that tells us what the sentence is about. The predicate includes all of the words and information that tells us what the subject is doing or what is being done to the subject.

A simple subject is the word, or small group of words, that is used to to signify specifically who the subject is. It is usually a noun or a pronoun.

The simple predicate is the singular word, or small collection of words, that completes the predicate part of the sentence. This is usually a verb.

Example:

1) The woman in the house cleans up the mess.

   Complete subject: the woman in the house // Simple subject: woman
   Complete predicate: cleans up the mess // Simple predicate: cleans

2) My young and hairy dog ran around the park

   Complete subject: My young and hairy dog // Simple subject: dog
   Complete predicate: ran around the park // Simple predicate: ran

Subject-Verb Agreement

Another rule of grammar is the agreement between the subject and the verb in a sentence. In this case, agreement means that the tense and characteristics of the subject is reflected by the verb of the sentence. For <u>instance</u> if the subject is plural then the verb must also be plural. Likewise if the verb is present tense, the subject has to reflect that.

Usually you will be able to hear that the subject-verb agreement is right. When it is <u>wrong</u> the sentence will not sound right when spoken.

Example:

'<u>I</u> sees you' is wrong as the verb does not reflect the tense of the subject.
'I see you' is correct.
'<u>They</u> sees you' is wrong // 'They see you' is right
'The Aliens flies the spaceship' is wrong // "The Aliens fly the spaceship" is right

Verb Tense

Verbs can generally be written in the past tense, present tense, or future tense. The past is meant for actions that have happened; the present is meant for actions that are happening now; future tenses are used for actions that will happen, but have not happened yet.

Under these three categories there are a number of specifications.

- Present perfect

  o This is used when an action began in the past and is continuing or still going on in the present.

Example- I have been scared of that movie in the past. They have had a fever since Monday.

- Simple present

  o This is used if the action is happening right now or it happens on a regular basis.

Example- I feel great right now! She loves cake!

- Present continuous

  o This is used when an action is happening now and will continue to happen in the future.

Example- They are changing the light bulb while we clean the house. They are standing over there waiting for us.

- Past Perfect
- Simple past
- Past continuous

- Simple future
- Future perfect
- Future continuous

Noun-Pronoun Agreement

Just as the subject and the verb have to be in agreement with each other, so does the noun and pronoun. This agreement is when a proper noun is used, its antecedent - that is the noun that is used following but referring to the same subject - have to make sense with each other.

Noun and pronouns can be in agreement through gender, through their singularity or plurality, and through their subject and object.

Example-

1) Agreement through gender.

   a) *Sasha* wore a red dress to the party. It was *her* favorite.
   b) *John* doesn't like green beans. *He* prefers broccoli.

2) Agreement through singularity and plurality.

   a) *The team* was very happy *they* won the tournament.

b) *Michael* woke up late for school and *he* missed the bus.

Parallel Structure

When it comes to grammar, parallel structure means when two or more sentences or clauses have the same structure. Using this can help make your writing more effective, clearer, and impressive.

For instance if you are listing some items and you are putting an adjective before one, then you should put an adjective before all of them. Or if you are describing one action in a series then you should describe every action.

> **Example-**
>
> Not Parallel- "We enjoy vegetables and grilled lamb chops.'
> Parallel- "We enjoy sauteed vegetables and grilled lamb chops.'
> Not Parallel- "He quickly ran away and hid behind the tree."
> Parallel- "He quickly ran away and quietly hid behind the tree."

Gerunds

A gerund is a noun that was made from a verb that has had -ing added to it. They are useful as they are another way to correctly present information without having to repeat or reuse the same sentence structure.

> **Example-** My doctor suggests meditating to help relieve my stress.
>
> *In this case suggests is the verb of the sentence and meditating is the noun or gerund.*
> Cooking and gardening are my passions.
> *In this case both cooking and gardening are gerunds*

Avoiding Fragments

Sentence fragments are a grammatical error, rather than a rule, and should be avoided. Fragments, when it comes to grammar, are when a sentence is not complete. A sentence needs to have a subject and a main verb or action to it. Without one, the other, or both, you will have a sentence fragment.

Example-

Fragment: The white snow /missing action / Full sentence: The white snow was falling.

Fragment: waiting for the bus /missing subject/ Full sentence: I stood in the snow, waiting for the bus.

Avoiding Run-on Sentences and Comma Splices

Almost as a direct opposite to sentence fragments, there are grammatical errors of run-on sentences and comma splicing. Many people think that a run-on sentence is just a really long sentence. But this is not necessarily the case. There are grammatically correct sentences that are long, and shorter sentences that are run-on sentences.

There are two forms of run-on sentences. The first is when the writer includes no punctuation or coordinating conjunction when connecting two clauses that are independent. The second kind of run-on sentence is called a comma splice. It is when just a comma is used to connect the two independent clauses.

Example-

Run-on sentence: The sea shells are beautiful you can hear the ocean in them.

Correction: The sea shells are beautiful. You can hear the ocean in them OR The sea shells are beautiful because you can hear the ocean in them.

Comma splice: The trees are tall, they provide shade to the park.

Correction: The trees are tall, and they provide shade to the park. OR The trees are tall; they provide shade to the park.

Commas

Commas are an incredibly common punctuation method in writing. In fact they are so common that they are often misused.

Clauses and Conjunctions

First, you should always use a comma when you are coordinating conjunctions and connecting two independent clauses.

Example-

I went to the park, and saw my friend.
I went to the party, but I didn't have fun.

Separating Items

One of the most common uses of a comma is to separate things in a list.

Example-

Yesterday I went grocery shopping and bought some apples, grapes, milk, and cheese.

There are some things to keep in mind when you are using a comma in this way;

1) A series is three or more items of the same kind. Two items can be separated by 'and' or another word. While a series of items of different kinds needs more punctuation.
2) The series still needs a conjunction like and, but, or, or before the last item.

Interjections and Non-Essential Information

Commas are also used to separate non-essential information in a sentence, or to add a dependent clause or phrase into an independent clause. Deciding what is essential and non-essential information will depend on the larger context of the piece.

> **Example-**
>
> It was too hot during the week, for anyone let alone for the kids, to play outside. *In this sentence, the information about the children was not needed*
>
> If you did go to the park, however, I hope you brought sunscreen and a hat.

Using Semicolons

Semicolons can be used to replace commas when coordinating conjunctions are at play in the sentence. Especially if you are using it to simplify an independent clause that uses many commas.

> **Example-**
>
> I am not feeling well. I have a cough, a headache, and a runny nose; but I will still go to work with you.
>
> You can also use semicolons to replace commas when you are listing items.
>
> **Example-**
>
> I love all kinds of fruit. I like berries, such as blueberries, and strawberries; stone fruits like peaches, plums, and nectarines; and even citrus fruits like lemons, grapefruits, and oranges.

Apostrophe Usage

The apostrophe is one of the most misused punctuation notes. This is because it can be used in a number of different ways and places.

Possession

First the apostrophe can be used to show possession or who something belongs to.

Generally, to show possession the apostrophe comes after the last letter of the word and is followed by an 's'. This rule usually applies to words that already end in an 's'

> **Example-**
>
> *Emma's* bow, *Johnny's* bike, *Thomas's* house, the *bus's* wheel.
>
> **Exceptions-**
>
> - For nouns that are made plural by giving them a 's', the apostrophe comes after the 's'.

The *boys'* excitement

- When the word 'it' is used to show possession no apostrophe is used at all.

    The tiger stalks *its* prey.

Omission of Letters

Apostrophes can also be used when we drop letters from words when we create contractions. Specifically the apostrophe takes the place of the letter or letters that were removed.

> **Example-**
>
> They are -> they're
> I am -> I'm
> Should not -> shouldn't

Plurals

A final use for apostrophes is to use them when we create plurals of different work. This use of an apostrophe is not in itself a primary rule in grammar or spelling. Rather it acts as an exception to the rules of how to make words plural in general.

Usually an apostrophe is used to make a word plural when simply adding an s would make the sentence not make sense.

Example-

Mind your p's and q's.

You will notice all of the **A's** are circled. *Note In this sentence if there was no apostrophe after the a it would be presented as 'as', which in itself is its own word*

Writing Strategies

The following are a list of different strategies that you can take when it comes to writing. Note that with each different strategy there are a number of different ways you can go about doing it.

Prewriting

Prewriting includes anything that happens before you actually write and create your piece. There are a few different methods to go about prewriting.

1) Brainstorming. Brainstorming is the method and process of coming up with as many possible ideas and statements about the topic. You can either do this in a list format or in a chart. From here, you can group your ideas together in like kinds to help you format the structure of your piece of writing.

2) Free writing. Free writing includes setting a timer for a short amount of time- say 15 minutes- where you write as much as you can about your chosen topic without having to do any sort of research. You can include any knowledge, any questions you have about the knowledge, and anything you for sure want to include in your writing piece. This will help guide you with your research and writing.

3) Mind maps. Mind maps, also known as concept Maps, are one way of showing how different ideas are connected to one another. You would have your main

topic in the centre, and branch off of it some ideas or pieces of information. The more you think about your main topic, the more lines you will have coming from the centre. However, as you move along, you are likely to come up with ideas that aren't directly linked to your main idea, but to a supplementary idea. In this case, you would draw a line from the supplementary idea to your new idea. Eventually what you will get is a web of ideas with lines connecting several ideas together.

4) Outlining. Outlining is a more structured way of prewriting. It involves you organising your thoughts as you think of them. For example, you will come up with your main topic, then list supplementary ideas and facts by importance after it. In this way it will help you stretch your ideas about how to write your piece while also organizing your thoughts.

There are a number of other ways that you can perform your prewriting. However the above mentioned four ideas are the most common. Keep in mind that the goal in the prewriting stage is simply bringing together your ideas, what you already know about your topic, and what you need to find out.

Research

The research stage of writing is where you find information to back up what you already know, and to answer the questions and fill in your lack of knowledge.

You can search the web, a library, and a variety of other places. Depending on the level of education and professionalism required of your piece of writing, you may need to use formal databases and properly cite information you find.

Generally there are six steps to the research process.

1) Figure out what you need to know. If this step is skipped then your research will be all over the place.
2) Do a preliminary search just to see where the best place is to find the information you need.
3) Find the information.
4) Make notes based on the information you find.
5) Write your paper or your piece of writing.

6) Evaluate and cite your sources properly if necessary to do so.

Drafting

The drafting process is the initial writing of your piece. Fill in the information that you found where needed, and fill in with your own thoughts. It is good in this stage to simply write what you feel and not focus too much on editing. Focusing too much on editing while you write can ruin the flow of your writing and halt progression.

Revising

This stage of writing is when you can review what you've written and make sure the flow makes sense. You can catch minor spelling mistakes and move the structure of your piece around to better present the information.

Editing and Proofreading

It is in this stage of writing that formal edits and fact-checking occur. This is when you will make sure that every punctuation mark and capital letter is exactly where they need to be. This is where you will double-check your sources to make sure that they are associated with the proper pieces of information. When it comes to editing and proofreading it is highly recommended that you take some time away from the piece and return to it. This way you have fresh eyes to be able to catch any grammar or content mistakes.

Chapter Two: Summary and Key Takeaways: Writing Study Guide

This study guide was devoted to helping you further develop your writing skills. Let's look at some of the key points in summary here.

- Parts of Speech

    o Noun- Names a person, place or thing.
        - is divided into proper and common nouns

- o Verb- shows an action
    - can be in the present, past, or future tense
- o Adjectives- describes or modify the noun
- o Adverb
- o Prepositions- describes a person, place or thing to be in relation to something else
    - in relation with where, when, and in possession
- o Conjunction- when you bring together two clauses.
    - Either an independent with a dependent clause or, two independent clauses
- o Interjection- show strong feelings or emotions
    - can be their own sentence or a part of another one.

- Spelling Rules
- Clauses
- Grammar
- Commas
- Apostrophe Usage
- Writing Strategies

    - o Prewriting- the planning stage and brainstorming
    - o Research- Finding the information you need to fill your knowledge gaps on your topic
    - o Drafting- free writing your initial draft
    - o Revising- Initial rereading and rewriting of the piece
    - o Editing and Proofreading- formal edit and fact-checking

Now that we have covered writing skills, let us now turn to the mathematical skills required for the exam.

Chapter Three: Mathematics Study Guide

The third chapter of this book covers topics on Mathematics for the ETS Praxis Examination, in which the third and the final section will be on the subject. It has the same weightage as the others. You have to go through the sections carefully and thoughtfully to help you round out your skills before you start practicing the lessons.

Number Concepts

Integers

Integer is a mathematical term derived from Latin, meaning intact or whole. This means that the integer is any *whole number*.

It cannot be a decimal or a fraction but can include positive and negative numbers. Zero is an integer. Z represents a set of integers.

Therefore, Z covers positive numbers above zero to negative ones below zero and zero. But ⅓ or 0.25 are not integers.

Examples of positive integers are 1, 2, 3 etc.; negative integers are written with a minus sign before the numbers and can be expressed as: -1,-2,-3, etc.

Zero or 0 is neither positive nor negative. It is a whole number, and so are the positive integers.

Therefore, a given set of Integer or Z = {-4,-3,-2,-1,0,1,2,3,4} and so on.

However, in mathematics, negative integers are called just that. Zero and the positive integers are called whole numbers. The positive integers above zero are also called natural numbers. Thus we may say, integers can be negative or whole. Whole numbers include zero and natural numbers like 1,2,3 etc.

You can also use a number line to represent a set of Integers visually. In the imaginary line, which is infinite and extends horizontally in both directions, left and right, you can place the numbers at an equal gap. The negative numbers are on the left, and the positive numbers are on the right.

-5 -4 -3 -2 -1 0 1 2 3 4 5

The negative integers Natural numbers or positive integers.

Zero is a whole number, neither negative nor positive, and occupies the central position in a number line. Natural numbers are also whole numbers. The numbers greater than zero are on its right side and are positive. The numbers lesser than zero are on its left side and are negative.

A number line, as is schematically given above, is used for mathematical calculations. If you are to place integers on a number line, remember that numbers on the right-hand side are always greater than those on the left-hand side.

Operations With Integers

Integers are used for addition, subtraction, multiplication, and division. Before we go into the rules for the operations, we need to remember a few important points. They are;

- No sign before a number implies it is positive. Thus 3 means it is +3.
- The *Absolute Value* of an integer comes without any sign negative (-) or positive (+). Thus, the absolute value of $|-4|$ =4, and the absolute value of $|4|$ =4.

When it comes to using integers in mathematical equations, usually when an integer is in an equation of any sort with other integers, the result will always be another integer or whole number. There are some exceptions to this rule; for example with division.

Critical Numbers

A critical number is the point in a series of numbers where it changes. For example, a series of numbers such as 1,2,3,4,5,4,3,2,1: 5 would be the critical number as it is there that the series of numbers changes.

Usually critical numbers are represented on graphs where there are curved lines and slopes that have to be calculated. The critical number would be at the point where a slope changes from positive to negative. To conceptualise it visually, the critical number would be the point at which the curved line changes from one direction to another.

Rational Numbers

A rational number is any number that can be written as p/q, and where q does not equal 0. In other words it is any fraction where the denominator is not 0. What's more is that a rational number is when the fraction can be divided and the result is represented in decimal form.

$\frac{1}{4}, \frac{1}{5}, \frac{8}{16}$

Rational numbers have an opposite; irrational numbers. Irrational numbers are numbers that cannot be shown or written as fractions.

Basic Math Functions

Addition

Addition is a procedure of adding two integers. Addition is when you take two or more numbers, and bring them together to combine their sums into one total sum. The answer in any addition is called a sum.

Depending on the numbers, positive or negative, their sum total can increase or decrease.

We may have either of two instances:

- The integers may have the same sign. Here you need to add the absolute values of the integers to get their sum. The sign of this new number will be the same as the individual integers.

To add you need only to count from your initial number the amount of numbers given to you by the second number.

Example: 2+ 3

Start at 2 and count up three numbers, 3,4,5 - The last number is your answer.

Words that signify or indicate that an addition has taken place include; plus, in addition to, the sum of which, and.

Addition equation as a sentence:

Six apples **plus** four apples equals ten apples

Addition equation as integers;

6 + 4 =10

Adding multiple number integers

When adding integers that have multiple numbers you will want to do it vertically.

1) stack the smaller number on top of the larger number
2) make sure that the last digit of each number is on top of each other with the others following.
3) Add each number choose the number that is directly above it
   a) if the resulting number is more than 10, carry forward the ten to the next additional pairing.
      - In the second instance, we may have an *addition equation with one posi-*

tive and one negative integers. In this case, *instead of adding* the absolute values of the two integers, we **subtract** to find the difference between the two numbers. Look at the example below to follow:

Example: Add two fingers of value 3+(-4)

We know that the absolute value of 3 and (-4) are 3 and 4, respectively. The difference between the absolute value of the two numbers is 4-3=1

The answer is 1 but what sign will you put before it? Look at the bigger value. It is 4, and it bears a negative sign before it.

Therefore, you will put a minus sign before 1 to indicate a negative value of the resultant number.

We may write the equation, 3+ (-4)= -1

- Things to remember when adding

    o   Any number added to 0 results in itself.
    o   Adding one to any number simply results in the following number.

Addition can be easily done with a number line. Here, the rules are that you start from the center, or 0. Go to the left of 0 if the integer is negative and go to the right of 0 if the integer is positive.

Example: Find the value of 5+(-7) using the number line.

-7 -6 -5 -4 -3 -2 -1 0 1 2 3 4 5

To solve the equation, we consider the positive or the bigger number first. It is 5. We must start from the center, which is the position of zero (0). How many steps (units) do you need to go to reach 5? You need to move 5 units.

Next, we move on the number line toward the left side, which is the domain of negative numbers. We go from 5. How many steps (units) do we need to move to reach -7 on the negative side? We need to move 12 units. Since we are moving to the left, we will put a minus sign before 12 or -12.

Your answer is -12.

Subtraction

Subtraction is a procedure *of finding the difference* between two or more integers. The value can *increase* or *decrease* depending on the integers, *negative* or *positive*. The number that is subtracted is called the subtrahend, and the number it is subtracted from is the minuend. The result is their difference.

In the example, 10 - 7 = 3, 10 is the minuend, 7 is the subtrahend, and 3 is the result of subtraction.

It is done by the following methods:

- You may change the sign of the subtrahend and convert the operation into an addition.
- Next, apply the same rules of addition of integers and solve the problem.

Example: Subtract the two integers, 5 and –10

Solution:

First step is to convert the operation to an addition problem. Doing that, we get: 5 + (–10).

In the next step we follow the same rules as for the addition of two integers.

The absolute values of the two integers are 5 and 10, respectively.

Their *difference* is: larger number –smaller number 10–5 =5.

But since the larger number 10 sports a negative sign before it, we will apply a negative sign before the result.

Therefore, the value of 5–(–10)= –5.

Multiplication

It is a basic mathematical function where you have to find the result of combining groups of things of equal sizes. Suppose there are four groups of three pens, and you need to know the total number of items you have. You can arrive at the solution by adding, which is time consuming or by multiplying.

✏✏✏=group1

✏✏✏=group2

✏✏✏=group3

✏✏✏=group4

To add all the pens, you will need to write the equation as 3+3+3+3=12.

To multiply, consider there are 4 groups, and each group has 3 pens. Therefore, there are 4 times 3 or 4 groups ×3 pens =12 pens. We may say multiplication is addition repeated.

It is denoted by ×, * (asterisk), or dot '.'. The number of things in each group is called the *multiplicand* (pens or 3 in the example above), and the number of common groups is called *multiplier (*the number of groups or 4 in the above example*)*. the result of multiplier and multiplicand is called the *product*.

Words that describe and indicate multiplication has taken place are; times, multiplied.

7 (multiplier) *4 (multiplicand) =28(product)

or 7+7+7+7=28

5 (multiplier) *10 (multiplicand) =50 (product)

or, 5+5+5+5+5+5+5+5+5+5=50

Multiplication can also be done with the help of a number line.

0 1 2 3 4 5 6 7 8

If we are to multiply 2*3, then remembering 2 groups (multiplier) times 3 objects (multiplicand), we move twice, each time jumping on three objects (Numbers). Let us start from 1. Jump over 3 objects (numbers) to reach 3. So, on our first jump, we reach number 3. Jump again, and you reach 6. The product is 6.

Multiplication Properties

In reality, when we are multiplying two numbers, the position of the multiplicand and the multiplier does not matter. Even when you interchange their places, the result will be the same. This is called commutative property.

Thus, a*b=b*a

Associative property: For numbers (a*b)*c=a*(b*c).

An example: if a=3, b=2, and c=2; then the equation is (3*2)*2=3*(2*2)

or, (6)*2=3*(4).

The result is 12 in both equations.

Distributive property: For numbers a*(b+c)=(a*b)+(a*c).

For example, if a=3, b=2, and c=5, then the equation can be written as

3*(2+5)=(3*2)+(3*5).

Or, 3*7=6+15

Or, 21 is the result on both sides.

Tips for multiplication

- If you multiply a number by zero, the product is 0
- if you multiply a number by 1, the product is the same as the number

Division

Division can be considered as you share your things fairly among your friends.

For example, you have 14 pens, and you want to distribute them among 7 students. How many pens should each student get? The answer to this question is obtained by division.

14÷7=2.

Each student will get 2 pens.

The division is the splitting or separating of numbers into equal parts. The division is identified by a ÷ or by a slash symbol: ' /'.

Words that indicate that a division has been made include; divided, separated, and shared.

The number that is being divided is called the *dividend*.

In the above example with the pens, 14 is the dividend.

The number dividing the dividend is called the *divisor*; in example 7, the number of students you have is the divisor. After division, the result obtained is called the *quotient*.

The example can be re-written as 14 (dividend) ÷ 7 (divisor) = 2 (quotient).

You may consider division the opposite of multiplication.

For example, in the multiplication of two numbers 3 and 6, the result is 3*6=18.

You may interchange the position of the numbers. The multiplication or 'product' of the two numbers 3 and 6, will be the same.

In the case of division, we use *the product as the dividend*. The divisor is the number we use to divide the dividend. Let us choose 3 as the divisor.

18÷3=6. The result or quotient is 6.

You may also choose 6 as the divisor; the result or quotient, in that case, will be 18÷6 or 3.

When you know the multiplication table, you can easily divide numbers.

For example, let us go through the multiplication table of 7.

7*1=7

7*2=14

∴**14 is 2 times 7.**

Another way of considering division is how many times does the divisor go into the dividend equally?

Sometimes division is not so easily finished.

We may have numbers and items left over from the division.

For example, if I have 9 chocolates and I'm dividing them between two friends, each friend can get 4 chocolates. and there will be 1 left.

9/2 = 4+4 +1. You may certainly keep that chocolate for yourself, and it is called the *Remainder*.

Another example with remainder can be 14÷3=4, with 2 as remainder.

Let us rewrite the equation with the numbers 4*3=12. But the dividend was 14. So, two things don't add up, and that is your remainder from the division.

Fractions

Fractions are numbers that represent a part of a whole.

Julie has called over 5 friends for her birthday party. Julie's mom bought her favorite chocolate cake. She cuts it into ½. She cuts this again into 6 equal pieces and gives each of the children a piece including Julie. We know that each of the children gets 1/12th of the cake. We are still left with the other 1/2 of the cake intact. Perhaps Julie's thrifty mom will keep it for another day.

We use a fraction to show and communicate how much of the cake each piece is worth; how much of the cake has been eaten; or how much of the cake is remaining.

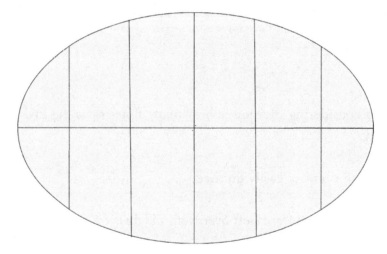

In the above schematic representation of the cake, you find the cake is divided horizontally into ½. Then I have intentionally divided each half into six equal parts to show you how much of the total cake each child received.

In this example, where fractions represent equal portions they are called equivalent fractions. In the example above, suppose Julie's mom divided the remaining half of the cake into six equal portions and ate one slice. She loved it and gradually ate up the other five slices as well. What she ate may not exactly look like half of the cake, but in effect, she ate ½ of it.

Therefore, ⅙+⅙+⅙+⅙+⅙+⅙=½. Please refer to the diagram above to understand.

Fractions have two parts that are divided by a slash. In the example with the cakes, the numbers are 1 slash 2 to indicate ½ of the cake.

The numerator is the top number above the slash. It represents the number of pieces in any specific problem, like how many pieces are left, how many pieces have been eaten, or how many pieces each person gets.

The denominator rests below the slash, and it represents how many pieces are in the whole.

If we have a cake and cut it into 6 pieces, then the denominator of any fraction would be 6.

Before any pieces are given out or eaten our fraction will read 6/6; because there are six pieces out of 6 pieces still available.

If there are six people at the party and each person receives one piece of the cake, then each person receives ⅙ of the cake. However if there are only 4 people at the party and each individual takes one piece then there will be 2/6th of the cake left over.

The denominator or the number below the slash representing the whole cake is 6. The numerator or the number of people present (4) to determine how many 'equal' portions the cake must be cut into, the fraction can be represented as 4/6. But the whole cake is 6/6. Therefore 2/6 of the cake is left over.

$$6/6 - 4/6 = 6-4/6 = 2/6.$$

Equivalent Fractions

Equivalent fractions are fractions that have different numerators and denominators from each other but represent the same value.

Let us use the example of the cake once more. This time we have two cakes. One cake that we have divided into six (6) pieces, and another that we have divided into twelve (12) pieces.

When both cakes are home they can be presented at 6/6 and 12/12. These two fractions are equivalent because they both represent 100% or 1 whole cake.

Now let's say that half of each cake is passed out. So 3 pieces of the cake that was cut into 6 is passed out, and six pieces of the cake that was cut into 12 pieces were passed out. Now each fraction can be written as the following;

3/6 and 6/12

Again both of these fractions are equivalent because they represent their respective cakes.

How can you derive an equivalent fraction from a given fraction?

You need to multiply the numerator and the denominator with the same number.

For example, 2/7 =2*3/7*3=6/21.

Let us consider this problem:

Find a fraction with a denominator of 28 that is equivalent to 4/7.

You multiply both numerator and the denominator with the same number. But, this cannot be any number. The denominator is 7. And you need to make it 28. Use the multiplication table to ascertain how many times of 7 is 28. You are right. It is 4.

Therefore, multiply both the numerator and the denominator with 4.

Or, 4×4 / 7×4=16/28.

The new fraction, therefore, is 16/28.

Let us consider another equation for equivalent fraction:

Blank/8 =3/24. You have to put a number in the position of the Blank. What will it be?

Find out from the multiplication table which number when multiplied with 8 gives 24.

It is 3. Since you <u>have to</u> work with the higher value of the fraction, you need to divide both numerator (3) and the denominator (24) with the same number i.e., 3.

3÷3/24÷3=⅛

Your answer is **Blank**=1

To crosscheck, you can multiply the numerator and denominator with 3; you will get 3/24 (*tlp-lpa.ca, 2022*).

Multiplying Fractions

Multiplying fractions is not a difficult process but does require multiple steps.

Unlike addition or subtraction of fractions where the denominator must be the same, with multiplication, fractions with different denominators can be multiplied.

The fractions should not be in the mixed form like 1⅓, they should be proper or improper fractions like 4/7 or 7/4. As the names suggest, a proper fraction is one with lower value in the numerator than the denominator; an improper fraction conversely, is one where the numerator is either equal to or greater than the denominator.

Let's multiply the fractions;

½ and 3/4

Step 1: multiply the two numerators together.

The numerators are 1 and 3 the product of which is 3

1 x 3 = 3

Step 2: multiply the two denominators together.

The denominators are 2 and 4 the product of which is 8

2 x 4 = 8

Step 3: simplify the fraction

Our new fraction is ⅜ .

Now we have to simplify. Crashed means to find the lowest possible denominator and lowest possible numerator while keeping the expression and value of the fraction intact. To simplify you have to find a number that both the numerator and the denominator can be equally divisible by.

For the case of our new fracture, ⅜, 3 cannot be equally divisible by any other number and therefore 3/8 is our lowest possible fraction and therefore does not need to be simplified.

Let's work with an example that does have to be simplified.

⅗ x 2/4

Step one: multiply the two numerators together

3 x 2 = 6

Step 2: multiply the two denominators together.

5 x 4 = 20

Step 3: simplify the fraction

6/20

6 can be equally divisible by 2 and 3

20 can be equally divisible by 2, 4, 5

Therefore both numbers can be divided by 2 which makes our new simplified fraction; simply divide both the numerator and the denominator by the same number.

6÷2/20÷2= 3/10.

The simplified fraction is 3/10.

The equation can now be written as 3/5 *2/4=3/10.

Indeed, the fraction 2/4 can be written as ½, a simplified version of 2/4.

Multiplying using visual model

This is a very easy and fast method to multiply fractions.

A

In this image of a square, you can see 4 columns, each of value ¼, and 4 rows, each of value ¼. Now, select a square that is common to both the columns and the rows. You are right. It is the first square marked with a bold A on the top. This block is 1/8th of the whole square.

Therefore, ¼*¼=⅛.

Multiplication of Mixed Fractions

How can you multiply 2⅗ * ¾?

You need to convert 2⅗ into an improper fraction. The steps for which are as follows:

Multiply 2 and 5. The product is 10.

Add 10 and the numerator of the fraction 3. The result is 13. Your improper fraction is 13/5.

In the next step multiply 13/5 and 3/4.

To do it, multiply the numerators 13 and 3. The product is 39.

Multiply the denominators 5 and 4. The product is 20.

Your resultant fraction is an improper one 39/20.

Since there are no factors common to 39 and 20, this is the simplified version. You can break it into a mixed form.

To do so, divide 39 and 20. The quotient is 1. The remainder is 19.

Therefore 39/20 can be written as 1¹⁹⁄₂₀

Multiplication With Same Denominators

The rule remains the same.

⅜*⅜=?

Multiply the numerators 3 and 3. The product is 9.

Multiply the denominators 8 and 8. The product is 64.

The fraction is 9/64 and it cannot be simplified further.

Multiply Different Denominators After Simplification

Multiply 2/8 and 6/9.

Now, 2/8 can be reduced to ¼ because they both have a common factor 2.

Similarly, 6/9 can be written as ⅔ because they both have a common factor 3.

Essentially 2/8*6/9 is therefore same as ¼*⅔.

The product is 2/12. This can be simplified again, because of the existence of the common factor 2. The answer is ⅙

2/8*6/9=1/6.

Cross check it.

Multiply the numerators 2 and 6=12.

The product of denominators is 8*9=72

12/72 has numbers 2,2,3 common between them. Their product is 2*2*3=12. Dividing the numerator and the denominator by 12 you get ⅙

Multiplying Fractions with whole numbers

Multiply 4 and ⅗

4 is really 4/1. Multiply this with ⅗

Multiply the numerators 4 and 3, the product is 12.

Now the product of the denominators is 1*5=5.

The fraction is 12/5. It is an improper fraction.

The mixed version is 2⅖

Multiplying Fractions With Mixed Numbers.

What will be the product of 2⅔ and 4⅗?

Convert both the fractions into imrpoer functions and carry on with the math.

8/3*23/5=8*23/3*5=184/15. Since this cannot be reduced anymore this is your answer. Note this is an improper fraction and can be converted to mixed fraction. The answer can further be modifies into 12⁴⁄₁₅

Tricks for easy multiplication

- Simplify the fractions before multiplication, if possible. Like 4/8 can be simplified as ½
- Simplification can be done across the fractions (*cuemath.com, n.d.*). Look at this example:

Multiply 3/18 and 4/10

In the first step, simplify both the fractions: ⅙ and ⅖.

In the next step, place the fractions side by side: ⅙, ⅖.

There is a common factor 2 between the denominator of the first fraction and the numerator of the second. They can be simplified: ⅙₃* ⅖ =1/15.

Adding and Subtracting Fractions

When the denominators are the same

When you have a set of fractions that have the same denominator, you need only to add the numerators together. Then put that new numerator on top of the original denominator.

Example:

5/10 + 4/10 = 5+4/10 =9/10 , because 5 + 4 =9.

The same principle is applied when subtracting fractions with the same denominator. Simply subtract the lower numerator from the larger numerator. The result will then be placed on top of the original denominator.

5/10 - 4/10 = 5-4/10 = 1/10, because 5 - 4 = 1

When the denominators are not the same

To add and subtract fractions with different denominators you first have to find the common denominator. The lowest common denominator is the lowest number that can be shared between two fractions as the denominator. In other words, the lowest common denominator is a number that both denominators can be a quotient for.

For example if we have the fraction 1/2 and ⅔ , the lowest common denominator would be 6 because both 2 and 3 can go into 6 equally.

2 x 3 = 6 and 3 x 2 = 6

Note that the Lowest Common Denominator or LCM can be greater than the existing denominators. Once this lowest common denominator is found, you have to convert denominators of both the fractions to express the LCM factor as their new denominator.

Multiply the denominators 2 and 3 with 3 and 2 respectively to get 6 as the common denominator for both the fractions. But when you multiply the denominator, you need to multiply the numerator as well with the same LCM factor. Because you cannot change the original value for the fractions.

Have a careful look:

½ = 1*3/2*3 =3/6$_2$ or ½ (the original value).

However, when you multiply only the denominator with 3 and keep the numerator unchanged, the fraction becomes ⅙, which was not the original fraction.

The two fractions will be expressed as:

½ x3 = 1*3/2*3=3/6

⅔ x 2 = 2*2/3*2=4/6

Now that both fractions have the same denominator, you can subtract or add them in the above mentioned way.

3/6 + 4/6 = 3+4/6 = 7/6

4/6 - 3/6 = 4-3/6 = ⅙

Let's use an example where it is not so easy to find a common denominator.

2/9 and 7/12

For this the lowest common denominator would be 36; 9 x 4 = 36 and 12 x 3 = 36.

How to arrive at it?

Write down the table of 9= 9, 18, 27, 36, 45, etc.

Write down the table of 12 till you find a match between the numbers 9 and 12.

Multiple of 12 are 12, 24, and 36.

The lowest number common to both 9 and 12 is 36.

There is a 'Common Division Method' by which you can find the LCM.

In this, you divide the numbers together with prime numbers and go on doing till they cannot be divided with any prime number.

```
2 | 9, 12
2 | 9, 6
3 | 9, 3
3 | 3, 1
    1, 1
```

So you get 2*2*3*3*1*1=36.

Now we have to do that to each fraction as a whole.

2/9 x 4 = 2*4/9*4=8/36

7/12 x3 =7*3/12*3= 21/36

Addition: 8/36 + 21/36 = 8+21/36= 29/36

Subtraction: 21/36 - 8/ 36 = 21-8?36 = 13/36

Order Of Operations

The word Operation with respect to Mathematics means in which order you must solve the problem. You will get a wrong answer for not following the order of doing the calculations. Therefore, mathematicians arrived at a rule with the mnemonic PEDMAS for you to do math operations.

Consider the equation 4+ (6*2^2+3).

Which part of the problem would you solve first? Do you start from the right or the left? Do you do the multiplication first, or solve the 'raised to the power of 2' first?

Indeed there are four basic equation types: addition, subtraction, multiplication, and division. When there is only one kind in each equation, it is easy to decide which operation and kind of equation to solve first.

4 + 4 + 8 = 16, 5 - 4 = 1, 2 x 3 = 6, 12 / 2 = 6

But what happens when there is more than one operator in the equation? Consider another equation:

(4 + 5) + (7 - 4) = ?

This is where the order of operations comes in. The order of operation is the order in which you should tackle the different operations in an equation.

The mnemonic PEMDAS is BEDMAS in Canada and BODMAS in the U.K. But the rules hold the same everywhere. Solve the P (or B) - parentheses or brackets first,

- Do any equation that is held within *brackets* or *parenthesis*; no matter the operation

  E- exponents

- Exponent is a number with a smaller number written in the upper right corner. It is an operation that asks you to multiply the number by itself that many times. It is expressed as 'to the power of"

  5 to the power of 3 = (= (5 x 5) x 5 = 5x5= 25 x 5 =125

  D- division

- Next you do any division that is not in a bracket

M- multiplication

- Next you do any multiplication that is not in a bracket

A- addition

- Next you do any addition that is not in a bracket

S- subtraction

- Next do any subtraction

Over time you will wittle the equation down until there is only one operation left.

Examples

Let us solve the first problem we encountered: 4+ $(6*2^2+3)$.

Remember that even within the Parenthesis, we must follow the rules of the operations. It means we do the exponents first, then the division and multiplication, and lastly, the addition or subtractions.

Solve the Parenthesis: within the parenthesis, there are multiplication, exponents, and addition. According to the rules of PEMDAS, we should tackle the exponents next.

$(6*2^2+3) = (6*4+3)$.

Next, solve the multiplication part: $(24+3)=27$. The parenthesis or the bracket is solved.

Next, we do the addition outside of parenthesis since the latter is solved.

$4+27 = 31$ is your answer to the problem.

The second problem was:

$(4 + 5) + (7 - 4) = ?$

Solve the parenthesis first.

(4+5) =9 and (7-4) = 3

Since there are no other operations left except for the addition outside of the brackets or parentheses, we can solve the problem easily: 9+3 =12.

Let us check another one.

   a) 3^3 x 2 = ?

Do the exponent first. (3 x 3) x 3 = 27

Then do the last operation: 27 x 2= 54

Therefore 3^3 x 2 = 54

But how to solve the following equation? Here you will find the use of two different kinds of parentheses.

   b) {4 x (2+3)} - 2=?

Parenthesis can be indicated by round brackets ( ) enclosing the mathematical operations; curly brackets { } and box brackets [ ]. The rule with different types of parenthesis is to solve the round brackets first, then the curly ones, and finally, solve the box brackets.

In the above equation, do the round bracket first: 2+3=5

Then do the operation in the curly bracket: 4 x 5 = 20

Then do the last operation: 20-1= 19

Therefore {4 x (2+3)} - 2= 19

   c) (6 /2) + {(26 -5) x $(2)^3$+ 3)} =?

This one is a little tricky but let's follow the steps. The equation is not difficult to solve when you follow the steps closely.

Let's do all of the brackets to do the round brackets (parenthesis) first. There are two sets of operations enclosed in the round brackets. According to the rules, we should do the exponents first.

2^3 = 2x2x2 = 8

Now the equation is

(6 /2) + {(26 -5) x 8 + 3}=

Solve the division within the round parenthesis next.

3+ {(26-5) x 8+3}

Then, do the subtraction within the round parenthesis.

3+{21*8+3}

Now we should pay attention to the curly brackets since we have solved the round ones. Again, do the multiplication first.

3+ {168 +3}

Do the subtraction component of the parenthesis.

3+ 171

Do the last step of the equation, i.e., addition.

The answer is 174.

Algebra

Algebra is a branch of maths that uses specific rules, symbols, and letters to solve equations and represent mathematical problems.

The symbols used in algebraic equations are not fixed values; they change and are hence called variables. It is necessary to represent these variables with nonspecific symbols like a, b, c, x, y, z, p, q, r, etc. Therefore, the variables are a, b, c, p, x, etc.

These symbols are used to carry out different operations like addition, subtraction, multiplication, and division using arithmetic rules. The idea is to find out a value for the variables.

Therefore, an algebraic symbol represents an unknown or changing number within the equation, the value of which has to be solved or filled in. This is the basis of Elementary algebra. It deals with equations involving the variables x, y, a, b, etc. Depending on the expressions of the variables, an algebraic operation can be Linear, Quadratic, or Polynomial.

A linear equation can be written as

$ab + c$

or, $ax + by$

or, $ab + bc + ad$

Example of a quadratic equation is $ab^2 - c^3d + ad = 0$.

An example of a polynomial equation $a(p) = 2p^2 + 5p + 12$; it deals with variables, coefficients, and exponents. However, the integer exponent of the variables must be non-negative like x^2 and not x^{-2}.

All the other branches of Mathematics like calculus, trigonometry, and coordinate geometry use algebraic expressions. Hence, algebra as a core concept is more important to all branches of mathematics.

Algebraic Terminology

Algebraic Expression: an algebraic expression is a sort of mathematical representation or equation where there are variables or unknown numbers, no numbers, and operating symbols.

An expression differs from an equation because the equation works on one side of the = symbol. An algebraic expression requires individuals to work on either side of the equal to sign =.

Algebraic equation has the following components: Variables, Operator, Coefficients, and Constants. In the following equation, 5a+2=12, 5 is the Coefficient, a is the Variable, + is the Operation, and 2 and 12 are the Constants.

- Variables: These are alphabets used to denote an unknown number the value of which you need to find in the algebraic problem. Variables change as long as it is not written out in an equation, when it can be solved by algebraic operations.

  For instance, say x and y are two variables. It is not clear what their values are unless we write out an equation for them which can say, 3x+2y=13. We may say probably, x=1 and y=5 to give us the numbers 3 and 10 respectively, which when added will give us 13. Therefore we need the equation to find out what the variables are standing for.

  The variables can be simple expressions like a, b, x, y, p, etc. They can be more complex like a^2, b^3, x^8y, etc.

- Coefficient: A coefficient would be a number that is multiplied by an unknown variable. If we use the equation 5y + 6x + 8, the coefficients would be 5 and 6

  Let us consider another equation.

  7a + 9.

  7 and 9 are fixed values, and a is changeable (variable).

- Terms: The expressions 7a and 9 are called Terms. A term is a designated number or variable within an expression. Terms refer to "grouping together" of variables and numbers.

Within the term 4x, you will notice that 4x is a multiplication of 4 and x. Multiplication connects the number with the variable x. 4x grouped together is a term. Addition and subtraction separate the terms from one another.

For example, in the expression 5y + 6x + 8 the terms are 5y, 6x, and 8.

Like Terms: Like terms are terms that share a variable with the same exponent.

For example, $3y^4$ and $7y^4$ are like terms.

- Degree: A degree is a term for the sum of the exponents within the expression.

  Let's change the above expression slightly. $5y + 6x + 8^2$

  In this above expression the degree of 8 would be 2

  But let's change the expression once more. $5y + 6x + 8^2 + 7x^4 y^3$

  For this new expression, the degree of 8 is still 2, but the degree of 7 is 7.

  If there is no exponent associated with a term, the degree of that term is 1.

  We may now look closely into different types of algebraic equations.

Linear Equation

A linear equation shows us the relationships among the variables like a, b, c, d, etc. They are presented in exponents of one degree. We do fundamental algebraic operations like addition, subtraction, etc., using the linear equation. Since we may have to solve them, let us understand them better.

Definition: A linear equation is an expression in Algebra where each term has an exponent of 1. When we plot a linear equation on a graph, we always get a straight line. Hence, it is called 'linear.'

The highest power a variable can have in a linear equation is 1, hence it is also called a one-degree equation. A typical example of such an equation is

$Ax+C=0$. Here A is a coefficient, C a constant, and x is the variable. This is an instance of an equation with 1 variable; an equation with two variables can be written as:

$Ax+By=0$, where x and y are the two variables.

Note $x+3y=7$ is a linear equation but $3x^2+y=0$ is a non-linear equation where the variable has power more than 1.

A linear equation formula can be expressed in various ways.

Standard Expressions

    i) $Ax+B=0$

    ii) $Ax+By=P$

These are two examples of general form of linear equation where A, and B are coefficients of x and y and P is a constant; x, and y are the variables.

Let us solve a standard linear equation with one variable.

    i) $3x + 2 = 11$.

To solve, $3x = 11 - 2$

$3x = 9$

Or, $x = 3$.

The second method is by placing a number on the left side of the equation to reduce $3x + 2$ to $3x$. The number is -2

$$\therefore 3x + 2 - 2 = 3x. \textbf{ (Solving the left side)}$$

but to balance the equation, you have to place -2 on the right hand side as well.

$$\therefore 11 - 2 = 9 \textbf{ (Solving the right side).}$$

So the equation can be rewritten as $3x + 2 - 2 = 11 - 2$

Or, $3x = 9$

Or, $x = 3$.

Example, i) Sum of two numbers is 10. One of the numbers is 7 less than the other. use linear equation to find the numbers.

Let the greater number be x.

We may write the equation as $x - 7 = 10$.

using the substitution method,

$x - 7 + 7 = 10 + 7$

Or, $x = 17$. Therefore the numbers are 17 and $17 - 7$ or, 10.

Numbers are 17, and 10.

ii) Seven times a number is 49. Find the number.

Let the number be x.

$7x = 49$

$x = 49/7$

x = 7.

The number is 7.

Linear equation Graphs

if the linear equation is with one variable, x forms a vertical line parallel to y-axis and vice-versa. If the equation has two variables, the graph is a straight line.

To plot a graph for equation x - y =2, do the following steps.

Express the value of y in terms of x.

$\therefore$ **y = x -2.**

Replace the value of x with different numbers to find out the resulting value for y.

Let x=0, then y= -2

If x is 2, then y is 0.

If x is 4 then y is 2

And if x is -2, then y is –4.

All these pairs of values for x and y satisfy the given equation, y = x - 2

List the coordinates now.

x   0   2   4   –2

y   -2   0   2   –4

We plot (4,2), (2,0), (0, -2), and (-2, -4) on a graph, joining the points in a straight line.

Quadratic Equation

A typical quadratic equation can be written as $ax^3 + bx^2 + c = 0$, where a, b, and c, are Constants. x is the variable. The value for x that will be required to solve the equation is called the Solution. A linear equation can have at most two Solutions.

Cubic Equations

As the name suggests, the variables have the power 3as exponents. A cubic equation has many applications in calculus and three-dimensional geometry.

$px3 + qx2 + rx = 0$ is a cubic equation example.

Sequences

What is a sequence in Algebra? An algebraic sequence, also called arithmetic sequence, refers to a sequence of numbers where the difference between *every consecutive term* is the *same*.

The difference is known as the '*common difference.*' To define sequence, we should know the first term of the sequence and the common difference *(cuemath.com, n.d.)*.

The formula for sequence defines the terms in the sequence. The formula is applied to find the nth term of an arithmetic sequence, provided the first term and the common difference between the terms are given. It can be written as follows.

$$a_n = a + d(n-1)$$

a_n is the nth term of the algebraic sequence. The first term should be a_1 or a. The addition sign indicates the term position, +, and the common difference is d.

Let us do a sum on this problem.

i) Find the 32nd term of an algebraic sequence 2, 4, 8, 12…

Here, a=2.

d= (4–2) = (8–4) = (12–8)=4

n=32

Now, apply the formula a_n = a + d(n-1)

a32 = a + d(n–1)

Substitute the variables with numbers.

a32 = 2 + 4 (32–1)

a32 = 2+ 4×31 (PEMDAS says you solve the parenthesis first).

a32 = 2 +124

Or, 126 is the 32nd term in the sequence.

ii) Find which term is 0 in the algebraic sequence 147, 140, 133, 126…

To find nth term which should be 0.

a = 147

Common difference d = (140–147), (133 –140), (126 –133) = –7

Our formula is an = a + d(n-1), and in this instance, an = 0 (given).

0 = 147 + (–7) (n –1)

Or, –147 = – 7 (n –1),

147/7 = (n–1),

21 = n-1

Or, n- 1= 21

n= 22

The 22nd term of the given sequence is 0.

Geometry

Geometry is a branch of mathematics concerning shapes, angles, dimensions, and sizes of various things we commonly see around us. Since it encompasses a vast number of things, we should learn about its terms before we can solve the problems.

Geometry Terms

- Point: A spot or a dot to indicate the exact position; it has no dimensions like length, breadth, or width. Example, Point A •
- A collection of points on a straight path that can extend infinitely in both directions is a line. For example, AB below is a line between two points A and B. A segment of line is between the two End Points on the line. AB in the picture is a line segment.

  A•_____•B

- 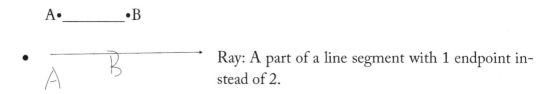 Ray: A part of a line segment with 1 endpoint instead of 2.

Imagine this line segment where points A and B on the line are open-ended.

- Angle: two Rays combine with a common endpoint to form an angle. The common endpoint is the Vertex, the two line segments are the Arms. When a ray is rotated about its endpoint, the measure of its rotation is the angle formed between its initial and final position.
- Triangle is a space enclosed by three lines.
- A polygon is a two-dimensional space enclosed by many lines; a triangle is a polygon and expresses the minimum number of sides a polygon should possess.

- A circle is a two-dimensional space enclosed by constituent points that lie at an equal distance from the center point. Only the points that make the border of a circle are of interest. Any point inside, also called interior points, does not make the circle

Triangles

Triangles have three arms, and they can be different shapes.

Equilateral triangle has all three sides equal, and all its angles are equal 60°.

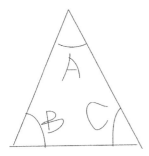

All its angles A, B, and C measure 60°.

A **Scalene triangle** is one with no sides, and hence, no angles equal.

An **isosceles triangle** has two equal sides. The angles opposite to these sides are therefore

equal. For example, in an isosceles triangle ABC, AB = AC.

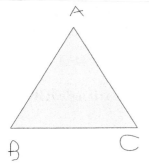

∠B = ∠C.

A **Right angle triangle** has one of the angles 90˚

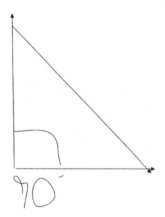

An **Obtuse angle triangle** has one 180˚.

An **acute angle triangle** has all its angles less than 90˚.

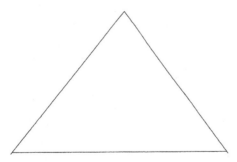

The perimeter of a triangle is the measurement of the sum of all three component sides. Its unit is the same as the unit of the sides.

∴ if AB = 5cm, BC = 6cm, and AC = 2cm, the perimeter of the triangle ABC is 5+6+2 = 13cm.

Area of a triangle is the measure of ½ its base × height. To measure the area of the triangle mentioned above, with BC as the base of the triangle, the area should be ½ ×6×H, where H is the height. How to calculate it?

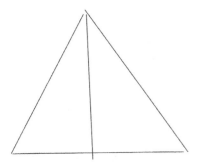

Drop a perpendicular line on the triangle base. This line is the height of the triangle.

Example, if the height of a given triangle is 8cms, and its base is 4cms, then what is its area?

Area = ½ base × height,

Or. ½ 4× 8 = 16cms.

If the height is unknown, but we know the sides of the triangle, we can find its area using Heron's formula.

s = (a+b+c)/2

where s = semiperimeter of the triangle.

A triangle with sides measuring 2cms, 4cms, and 6 cms has s = 2+4+6 /2 or

s = 6

The formula further says, Area A = √[s(s−a)(s−b)(s−c)].

∴ A = √[6 (6−2) (6−4) (6−6)]

A = √[6× 4× 2]

$=\sqrt{48} = \sqrt{[2\times2\times2\times2\times3]} = \sqrt{[2^22^23]}$. Or $4\sqrt{3}$

Properties of a triangle are as follows (*byjus.com, n.d.*).

i) The sum of all angles of a given triangle is 180°.
ii) The exterior angles of the triangle add up to 360°.
ii) Its shortest side is always opposite the smallest angle.

Polygons

A polygon is a two-dimensional geometric shape with a finite number of sides that encloses a space. The circle is not a polygon because it has no sides.

The slides of a polygon are straight lines that meet at each other's ends. The endpoint where two sides meet to form an angle is called the vertex. A minimum of three sides is required to enclose a two-dimensional space, and hence, a triangle is a polygon with three sides.

One with four sides is a tetragon, with five sides is a pentagon, and a hexagon is a polygon with six sides. A polygon with n-sides is a n-gon.

Types of Polygon

Regular Polygon

A polygon with all equal sides and angles. Examples are square, rhombus, and triangle.

Irregular Polygon

When all the sides and the interior angles of a polygon are different, it is called an irregular polygon. Examples are a kite, a scalene triangle, and a rectangular plot.

Convex Polygon

When all the interior angles of a polygon are less than 180°, it is called a convex polygon. The vertex points outwards from the center of the figure. V denotes the vertices of the convex polygon below.

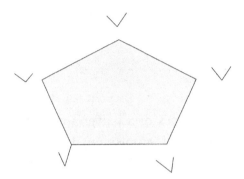

Concave Polygon

When *one* or more of the interior angles are more than 180°, it is called a concave polygon. The vertex points inwards.

 The marked angles are more than 180°.

Angles of Polygon

Angles of a polygon are 'exterior,' or those pointing outside, and 'interior,' or those pointing inwards.

Interior Angle Property

The sum of all the interior angles of a n-gon = (n–2) × 180°.

Or, (n – 2)π radians. n represents the number of sides of the polygon.

For example, for a quadrilateral with 4 sides, the sum of all its interior angles is as follows.

S = (4 −2)180°

S= 2 ×180°

S= 360°.

Exterior angle property

The sum of the interior and the exterior angles at each vertex of a polygon are supplementary to each other. Let us refer back to the value of supplementary angles, which is 180°.

∴ Interior angle + Exterior angle = 180°

Exterior angle = 180° − Interior angle

Properties of Polygon

- The sum of all the interior angles of a polygon with n-sides is (n–2) × 180°
- Number of diagonals of this polygon will be n(n – 3)/2
- If you join the diagonals from one corner to another, the number of triangles that will form is given by formula n – 2.
- The measurement of each interior angle is [(n – 2)× 180°
- For the exterior angle, the value will be 360°/n.

Area and Perimeter of Polygons

Area is the region enclosed by the sides of a polygon.

The perimeter is the total distance that the sides cover to enclose the area (*byjus.com, n.d.*).

It will be helpful if the area and perimeter formulae for different polygons are given in a table.

Name of Polygon	Area	Perimeter
Triangle	½ × Base × Height	A+B+C(A,B,C are the sides)
Square	Side× 2	4
Rectangle	Length × Breadth	2 (Length + Breadth)
Parallelogram	Base × Height	2 (sum of the pairs of the adjacent sides)
Trapezoid	½ × (Sum of parallel side) × Height	Sum of all sides
Rhombus	½ × product of diagonals	4 × Side
Pentagon	$1/4\sqrt{5}(5+2\sqrt{5}) \times (side)^2$	Sum of all five sides
Hexagon	$3\sqrt{3}/2 (side) \times 2$	Sum of all six sides

Quadrilateral

As the name suggests, a quadrilateral is a two-dimensional space within four sides. Squares, rectangles, kites, and trapezoids are examples of quadrilaterals.

Properties

A quadrilateral has 4 sides, 4 corners where the sides meet (vertices), and its interior angles add up to 360°.

Types

Rectangle: All angles are 90°, and the opposite sides are equal and parallel to each other.

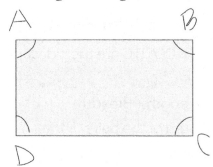

AB = DC, and AD = BC. ∠A, ∠B, ∠C, ∠D = 90°. AD ⌐ BC, AB ⌐ DC

Square: All angles 90°, and all sides are equal, note each corner of a square is at a right angle. Its opposite sides are parallel to each other.

Rhombus: Also called a rhomb, or a diamond, all the sides of a rhombus are equal, the opposite sides are parallel, and opposite angles are equal. The diagonals of a rhombus cut each other (bisect) at a right angle in the center.

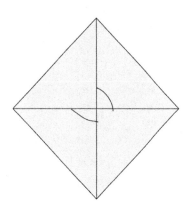

Parallelogram: The opposite sides are equal and parallel. Its opposite angles ∠A are equal.

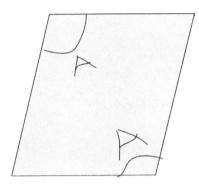

Trapezoid: One of its opposite sides are parallel. A Trapezium on the other hand has no parallel sides.

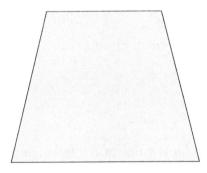

Kite: Adjacent pairs of sides are equal. The angles where the two pairs meet are equal. The diagonals meet at right angles bisecting each other.

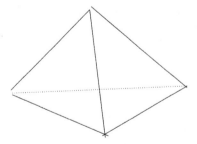

Note that a square, a rectangle, and a rhombus are also called parallelograms by some mathematicians. Note also that the square is the regular quadrilateral and the rest are irregular. Therefore, a square is a type of rectangle, but a rectangle is not a kite.

To understand this, let us look at the family tree of the quads.

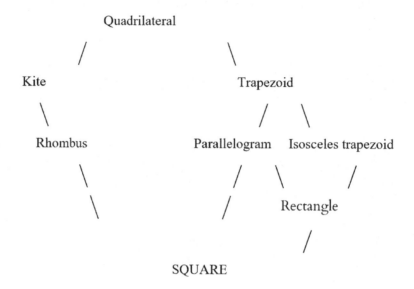

A quadrilateral is a polygon, since it encloses a space (*mathsisfun.com, n.d.*).

Circles And Circular Measurements

You may consider a circle as a hula hoop. All the points on the rim of the hula hoop make a circle.

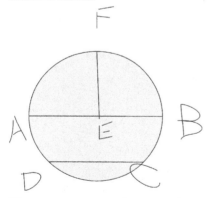

This is a picture of a circle, where AB is called **diameter**. It has endpoints A and B on the border and the line segment AB passes through the center of the circle.

The line EF that goes from the center E of the circle to the border point F, is the **radius** of a circle. It is ½ of the diameter.

A line segment with endpoints D and C on the border but not passing through the center of the circle is called a **chord**.

The distance the border travels to make a circle is called the **circumference**. It is denoted by C.

C = 2πr, where r is the radius.

You can see that C = πd where d is the diameter of the circle because we already know that 2π=d. The value for π is 22/7 or 3.141592

You can also see that circle since it comes round to where it starts forms a 360°. A circle can be divided by the **arc** in smaller sections. For example, if you follow endpoint D on the circumference until C, you will inscribe an arc of a circle. The name of the arc depends on the angle it forms.

We measure the arc of a circle in degrees ° or radiansπ.

π An arc of a circle can be 90° or π/2 when we are talking about a quarter of the circle.

If on the other hand, we refer to half of the circle, we mention the arc angle as 180° or π. It is half of the circle. Note that an arc of a circle is always less than 360°, or 2π which is the circumference of the circle.

The angles can be minor arcs (0° < v < 180°), or major arcs (180° < v < 360°), and semicircles v =180°.

The length of an arc, l , is determined by the following formula.

l = C· (circumference of the circle)

v (measure of the arc)

360

l = C· v 360

In the picture of the circle, you could see that two diameters will meet at the center to form central angles. It is like cutting a cake into pieces.

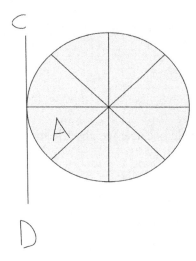

The circle is divided into eight equal pieces with the same angle as is shown in this diagram. Each slice is called a **sector**. ∴ A is a sector in the picture.

Tangent is a line that touches the circle at one point only. It is perpendicular to the radius. In the picture, CD is a tangent.

Example, The circumference of the circle is 10 length units. Find out the length of the arc of each piece.

We have to determine the angle for each piece first. We know that a full circle is 360°. therefore, the angle for each piece will be 360/8 = 45°

Applying the values to the formula,

l = C· v 360

l = 10·

45

360

= 1.25

l = 10·45360 = 1.25

The length of the arcs <u>are</u> 2.5 length unit. We could achieve the result easily by dividing the circumference 10 with the number of the same sized pieces 8.

∴ 10/8 = 1.25

Formulas for Circle Measurements

i.   C = 2πr or πd, where C is the circumference, r is the radius, and d is the diameter. π is a constant value, amounting to 22/7

ii. Area of a circle A = πr²

iii. Central angle π= 360 l/2π r, where l is the length of the arc.

iv. Inscribed angle is formed by two chords and a vertex on the circumference, and it is equal to one half of the measurement of the intersected arc (*math10.com, n.d.*).

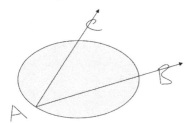

Let us say, the arc CB measures 80°, the measurement of the inscribed angle CAB is 80/2 or 40°.

v.   Angle between secants: They are the line segments that intersect each other *inside* the circle.

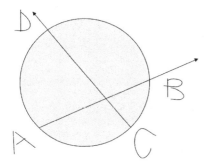

a) Let us say that the arc AD is 60° and the arc BC is 40°. The angle between the two secants is calculated as 60+40/2 or, 100/2 = 50°

vi. If the two secants intersect outside the circumference, the angle formed is half of the difference between the two arcs, or 60 - 40/2 = 20/2 = 10°

vii. Intersecting chords: the two chords AB and CD, meeting at a point X (imagine) inside the circle.

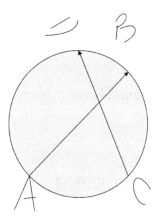

AX·XB = CX · XD

viii. Area of a sector = $\theta/2 \cdot (r^2)$.

ix. Area of a circular ring inside the circle of radius r is

$\pi(R^2 - r^2)$, where R is the radius of the original circle.

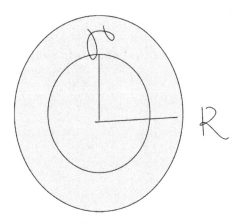

Three Dimensional Shapes

A three-dimensional shape in geometry is a solid figure or a shape with three dimensions, length, breadth, and height. It has a thickness or depth that makes it different from a two-dimensional thing.

Examples of a three-dimensional figure are a cone, a pyramid, a sphere, and a cube (*splashlearn.com, n.d.*).

A 3-D shape has faces, edges, and vertices.

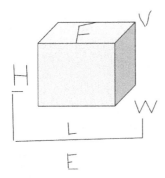

F = Face, E = Edges, W = Width, H = Height, W = Width, V = Vertex.

Examples of three-dimensional shapes in real life are:

Cube - a dice has 6 faces (F), 12 edges (E), and 8 vertices (V).

Rectangular prism - a shoe box has 6 faces (F), 12 edges (E), and 8 vertices (V).

Sphere - A ball with 1 curved face, 0 edges, and 0 vertices

Cone - A carrot, or ice cream has 1 flat face, 1 curved face, 1 edge, and 1 vertex.

Cylinder - A pail with 2 flat faces, 1 curved face, 2 edges, and 0 vertexes.

Note, that all three-dimensional shapes are made up of two-dimensional figures (*splashlearn.com, n. d.*).

Polyhedron

3-D figures with straight-lined solid figures are called Polyhedrons. They have straight edges, flat faces, and vertices. They are defined according to the number, shapes, and sizes of E, F, and Vs. A cube is a regular polyhedron with six faces, 12 edges, and eight vertices.

A tetrahedron has F 4, E 6, and Vertices 4. It is from a triangle.

An octahedron is also from a triangle and has F 8, E 12, and V 6

Dodecahedron has F12, E 30, and V 20. It is from a pentagon.

Icosahedron has F 20, E 30, V 12, from a triangle.

A prism has two triangle ends and three parallelogram sides with a total of 5 faces.

A pyramid is a polyhedron with a polygon base and sides meeting at the top point or apex.

Regular polyhedrons are those having identical faces where each face is a regular polygon. Examples are

tetrahedrons, with 4 equilateral triangle faces.

a cube with 6 square faces

octahedron with 8 equilateral faces

a dodecahedron with 12 pentagon faces

icosahedron with 20 equilateral faces.

Curved 3-Ds

These are cylinders, cones, spheres, and torus (like inflatable swim floats) (*skillsyouneed. com, n.d.*).

Surface Area Calculation of 3-D figures.

Surface Area of a Cube

L*W*6, where L= length, W= Width, and 6 is the number of faces.

Since a cube has a square face, the L=W

Find the surface area of a cube with W = 5cm.

One face of the cube is L*W or, 5*5 =25 cm^2

A cube has 6 faces, hence the surface area is 25*6 =150cm^2

For other types of regular polyhedrons, find the area of one side and multiply with the total number of sides for the figure.

For a dodecahedron, for instance, with an area of one of its pentagons as 11cm^2, multiply by 12, the number of sides to get its surface area. 11*12 =132cm^2

Surface area of a cylinder

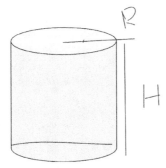

H is the height, and R is the radius. From the picture you can see a cylinder has 2 circles top and bottom, and a rectangle.

∴ Area of one circle is $\pi \times$ radius^2

The radius is say 2 cm, then the area of the circle is 3.14 $\times$ 4 =12 .56cm^2

The area of two circles will be 12 .56✕ 2 =25.12cm2

Next you need to find the area of the side of the cylinder = perimeter of the circle × the height of the cylinder.

Perimeter = π✕ 2×R. Or, 3.14 × 2 × 2 =12 .56.

Let us say the H is 6cm.

The surface area of the side of the cylinder is 12.56 × 6=75.36cm^2

Total surface area is 75.36 + 25.12 =100. 48cm^2

Surface area of a sphere

It is given by the formula 4× π× radius^2

Or, 4× π×d where d=diameter=radius^2

Surface area of a cone

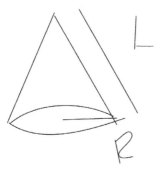

We need to know the values of length of the slant L and the radius R. Let the values be 6 and 2 respectively. A cone's components are the circle at base and a pyramid with a curved base.

Now consider the area of the circle at the cone base = π✕ radius^2

Or, 3.14× 2 × 2 = 12 .56cm²

Next, find the area of the slope = π×R L = 3.14 2 6 = 37.68cm²

∴ **The surface area of the cone is 12.54 + 37.68 = 50.22cm²**

Lines And Angles

Lines and angles are fundamental to geometry shapes.

Lines

All geometrical figures contain lines. It can be defined as a set of closely-spaced dots extending in both directions to infinity. A horizontal or a vertical mark on a piece of paper is a line. It is a 1-D figure with no width. In a cartesian plane a line is expressed by the linear equation, ax+ by = c

A•   •B

Since line AB has two endpoints, it is called a line segment.

A **ray** is a line which unlike the line drawn above has one end open to infinity. When two rays join at one of their ends, they form an **angle.**

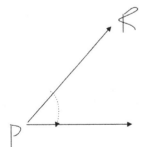

PR is a ray. The angle formed by the rays is shown with a dotted line.

Angle

Two rays meet at one of their ends to form an angle. They are expressed in degrees, denoted by °. It measures the rotation of the lines from the common endpoint, also called the vertex. The symbol is ∠ , and the value of an angle can be anything from 0° to 360°.

Types of Lines

Lines can be vertical, horizontal, or parallel to each other to keep the same distance throughout and not meet at any point.

Other types of lines are perpendicular and transverse.

- Parallel lines: When two lines do not meet with each other at any point and remain equidistant from each other. Symbolically, two parallel lines A and B are written as A∥B.
- Perpendicular lines: These are two lines that meet each other at right angles ⊥ where AB is the horizontal line, and CD is a vertical line. The lines AB and CD meet at right angles, 90°.
- Intersecting lines: These are two lines that intersect each other at exactly one point.

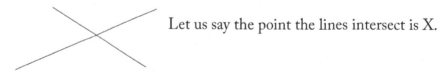 Let us say the point the lines intersect is X.

- A Transversal is a line that intersects two or more lines in a plane at different points.

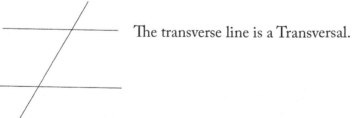 The transverse line is a Transversal.

Angle

Two Rays combine with a common endpoint to form an angle. The common endpoint is the Vertex; the two line segments are the Arms. When a ray is rotated about its endpoint, the measure of its rotation is the angle formed between its initial and final position.

Depending on the degree of rotation, the angles can be of different measurements.

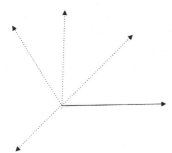

When the arms of the angle are perpendicular to each other, a Right angle is formed.

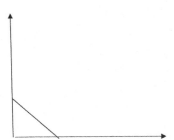

An Acute angle measures more than zero degrees 0° and less than ninety degrees 90°.

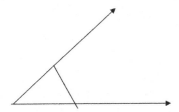

An Obtuse angle measures between ninety degrees 90° to one hundred and eighty degrees 180°.

The angle that measures 180 degrees (180°) is called a Straight angle. The curved drawing is the measurement of the angle.

An angle that measures more than one hundred and eighty degrees 180° and less than three hundred and sixty degrees 360° is called the Reflex angle. The curved arrow drawing indicates the angle formed.

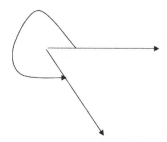

A Complete angle is formed when two arms overlap each other coming back full one circle around the common endpoint. It measures or equals three hundred and sixty degrees (360°) and is known as a complete angle.

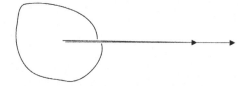

Complementary angles are formed when the sum of two angles adds up to 90°. Thus 45° + 45° will form a 90° angle. They are, therefore, complementary angles.

Supplementary angle: Supplementary angles form when the sum of two angles is 180°. Thus, 120° and 60° angles add to form a supplementary angle.

Lines And Angles Properties

- Lines and angles are 1-D geometric figures
- Lines are set of an infinite number of points spaced close to each other
- Lines extend in both directions infinitely.

- Lines have no depth or thickness
- Angles are formed when two lines intersect each other at an endpoint. It means that these two lines do not run parallel to each other and meet at a point.
- The lines that form an angle are called arms and their meeting point is the vertex (*cuemath.com, n.d.*).

XY Coordinate Plane

A coordinate plane is a 2-D figure formed by two intersecting number lines. The horizontal number line is the X-axis and the vertical number line is the Y-axis. The two lines intersect each other at right angles in a perpendicular plane which is called the coordinate plane.

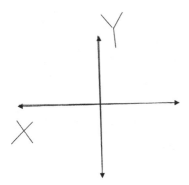

The number 0 is placed in the center of the two lines and is called the origin.

Positive Numbers from 0 onwards are plotted along the right-hand side of the X-axis and upper direction of the Y-axis.

Negative numbers from 0 downwards are plotted along the left-hand side of the X-axis and the lower direction of the Y-axis.

The plane is 2-D, any location on this plane is a matter of two things— distance from the X-axis and distance from the Y-axis. The plane is indeed used as a map to plot directions from one point to another.

Elements on a Coordinate Plane

Quadrants

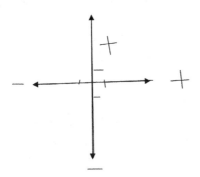

Let us consider four numbers on the X and Y axes equidistant from 0. They can be written as +1 and -1 on the X-axis, depending on whether they are on the right side or the left side of the origin 0.

The corresponding points on the Y-axis will be +1 and -1 depending on whether they are on the top or on the bottom segment of y axis from the origin 0.

We can see that the two number lines divide the coordinate plane into four sectors. These sectors or regions are called Quadrants. The quadrants are denoted by Roman numerals and each quadrant has its properties.

The upper right quadrant is quadrant I. Both x and y axes have positive numbers here.

The upper left quadrant is quadrant II. X has negative numbers and y axes has positive numbers here.

The bottom left quadrant is III. X-axis has negative numbers and Y-axis has negative numbers as well.

The bottom right is quadrant IV. The X-axis has positive numbers while Y-axis has negative numbers.

Coordinate

Every point on the coordinate plane is an expression in pairs of numbers x and y that show the position of the number on the plane with respect to the two axes.

Let us consider point A on the coordinate plane. To denote its position in terms of x and y we will write as follows.

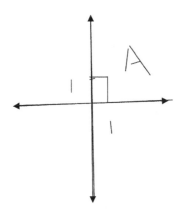

We find the location of point A with respect to the numbers on the two planes. On the X-axis it lies at +1 unit and with respect to the Y-axis, it lies at +1 unit again. This is written as the position of A in the coordinate plane is (1,1) (*splashlearn.com, n.d.*).

Inequalities

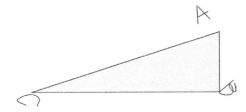

- Consider the triangle ABC. You can see that AC is more than the side AB. In this case, the angle opposite the longer side ∠B is always greater than the angle opposite the shorter side ∠A. Conversely when one of the angles is greater than another angle, ∠B > ∠A, then the side opposite the greater angle is longer than the side opposite the lesser angle, or, AC>AB.

- Note, that the sum of the lengths of any two sides of a triangle is always more than the length of the third side (*mathplanet.com, n.d.*).

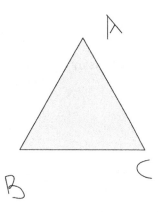

∴ AB + BC> AC

BC + AC >AB

AB + AC> BC

Measurements

We have different units for measurement in mathematics. For example, we measure the length in inches or centimeters and weight in kilograms or pounds. There are smaller units to measure smaller units. And we sometimes need to convert units into smaller or bigger ones. We may also need to convert units from one system, namely C.G.S., to another, namely, F.P.S.

There are three systems of units in mathematics.

- C.G.S: centimeter (cm), gram (g), and seconds (s).
- F.P.S: Foot (ft), pound (lb), and seconds (s).
- M.K.S: Meter (m), Kilogram (kg), and seconds (s).

For the sake of simplicity, we consider English and Metric systems.

English systems include feet, inches, pounds, and hours, and the Metric system includes kilometers, meters, centimeters, grams, kilograms, hours, seconds, etc.

Conversions

Kilometer/hour to meters/seconds = 1000/3600 = 0.2777m/s

1 Kilometer = 1000meters and 1 hour = 60*60 = 3600seconds.

Example:

Convert 6 kilometers/hour to meters /seconds.

6 kilometers is 6*1000meters or, 6000meters/sec

One hour needs to be converted to seconds. Hour is the bigger then seconds and one hour is = 60*60 seconds or 3600 seconds.

To write the formula, we may do the following.

3000/3600 = .30meters/second.

Conversion Tables

Table 1: Conversions within the same system

Metric to metric	English to English
Length:	**Length:**
1 kilometer (km)= 1000 meters 1 meter (m) = 100 centimeters 1 decimeter (dm)= 10 centimeters 1 centimeter (cm) = 10 millimeters (mm) 1 meter = 10 decimeter	1 Foot = 12 inches 1 inch = 2,54 centimeters 1 yard = 3 feet 1 yard = 36 inches

Weight:	**Weight:**
1 kilogram (kg) = 1000 grams 1 gram (gm) = 1000 milligrams (mg) 1 metric ton = 1000kg 1 gigagram = 1000 megagram 1 decagram =10 gram	1 pound (lb) = 16 ounces (oz) 1 ton (T) = 2,000 pounds (lb)
Capacity:	**Capacity:**
1 centiliter (cl) = 10 milliliter(ml) 1 decileter = 10 centileter 1 liter (l) = 1000 milliliters 1 liter = 10 deciliter 1 kiloliter (kl) =1000 liters (*byjus.com, n.d.*)	1 tablespoon = 3 teaspoons 1 fl oz = 2 tablespoons 1 cup (c) = 8 fluid ounces (fl oz) 1 pint (pt) = 2 cups © 1 quart (qt) = 2 pints (pt) 1 gallon (gal) = 4 quarts (qt) 1 gallon (gal) = 128 fluid ounces (fl oz)

Table 2: Other conversions

Metric system	English system	System conversion
Area:	**Area:**	**Area:**
$1cm^2 = 100\ mm^2$ $1dm^2 = 100\ cm^2$ $1m^2 = 100\ dm^2$ 1 are (a) =$100m^2$ 1 hectare (ha) = 100 are	1 square foot (ft2) = 144 square inches (in2) 1 square yard (yd2) = 9 square feet (ft2) 1 acre = 43,560 square feet (ft2) 1 square mile (mi2) = 640 acres	$1\ in^2 = 6.45\ cm^2$ $1\ m^2 = 1.196\ yd^2$ 1 ha = 2.47 acres
Volume:	**Volume:**	**Conversion from one system to another:**
$1\ cc = 1\ cm^3$ 1 milliliter (ml) = $1\ cm^3$ 1 liter (l) = 1,000 millimeters (ml) 1 hectoliter (hl) = 100 liters (ml) 1 kiloliter (kl) = 1,000 liters (l)	1 cubic foot (ft^3) = 1,728 cubic inches (in^3) 1 cubic yard (yd3) = 27 cubic feet (ft^3) 1 cord = 128 cubic feet (ft^3)	$1\ in^3 = 16.39\ mL$ 1 liter = 1.06 qt 1 gallon = 3.79 liters $1\ m^3 = 35.31\ ft^3$ 1 quart= 0.95 L

1 millisecond = 1,000 microseconds 1 second =1,000 milliseconds 1 minute = 60 seconds 1 hour = 60 minutes 1 day = 24 hours 1 month = 30 days 1 year = 365 days 1 banking year = 360 days	1 millisecond = 1,000 microseconds 1 second =1,000 milliseconds 1 minute = 60 seconds 1 hour = 60 minutes 1 day = 24 hours 1 month = 30 days 1 year = 365 days 1 banking year = 360 days (*mcckc.edu, n.d.*)	Temperature conversion from one unit to another: C°= 5/9 × (F-32) F° = 9/5 (C+32).

Table 3: Conversion from one system to another.

Metric To English	English To Metric
Length:	**Length:**
1 millimeter (m) = 0.04 inches 1 centimeter (cm) = 0.39 inches (in) 1 meter = 39.37 inches = 3.28 feet 1 meter = 1.09 yard (yd) 1 kilometer = 0.62 miles (mi)	1 inch (in) = 2.54 centimeters (cm) 1 foot (ft) = 30.48 cm = 0.305 meters (m) 1 yard = 0.914 meters 1 mile = 1.609 kilometers (km)
Weight:	**Weight:**
1 gram (gm) = 0.035 ounces (oz) 1 liter (l) = 1.057 quart (qt).	1 ounce = 28.350 grams (gm) 1 pound = 0.453 kilograms (kg)
Capacity:	**Capacity:**
1 milliliter (ml) = 0.2 teaspoon (tsp) 1 liter (l) = 1.057 quart (qt)	1 teaspoon (tsp) = 5 milliliters (ml) 1 cup (c) = 236 milliliters (ml) 1 quart (qt) = 0.9461 litre (l) 1 gallon (gal) = 3.785 liter (l)

Dimensional Analysis (Unit Factor Method)

This method of conversion assumes that any number or expression can be safely multiplied by 1 without any change in values. Although the value remains unchanged, it helps in changing the unit of measurement. The concept used is of equivalent values.

We use a conversion ratio or unit factor which is 1. The "ratio" bears the names of the units that will be used in conversion. We can use this system for conversions within a system, or for conversion of an unit of one system to another unit of another system.

For example, how do we convert 1 foot to 1 inch? Conversion ratios are always equal to 1.

It means to convert 1 foot to 1 inch, both numerator and the denominator should measure values of 1.

Using this principle, we may write the conversion ratio as follows.

∴ 12 inches/12 inches =1

Or, 1 foot/12 inches

∴ 1 foot = 12 inches.

The **conversion ratio** must have the **unit you want as the numerator** and **the unit you already have as the denominator.**

Dimensional Analysis set up pattern

$$\text{number of units you have} \times \frac{\text{units you want}}{\text{units you have}} = \text{number of units you want.}$$

Or,

$$\text{number of units you have} \times \frac{\text{unit you want}}{\text{unit you have}} = \text{number of units you want.}$$

Calculations may not be always simple and you may have to do it in more than one step. You have to persist with the cancelations until only the desired unit remains. All conversion ratios should be 1.

Let us do a few sums to understand how the system works.

The first example is conversion within the system, the second conversion from one system to another.

Example: i) Convert 5.5 kilometers to millmeters.

unit you want (millimeters)

number of units you have (5.5km) × _____ = number of units you want.

unit you have

1,000,000 mm

Or, 5.5 km ×_____ = 5,500,000mm

1 km

Example ii): Convert 45 miles per hour to feet/second

5280 feet   1 hour   1 hour

45 miles ×_____ ×_____ ×_____

1 mile   60 mts   60seconds

Or,

45* 5280/3600 = 66 feet/second.

Perimeters and Circumference

Perimeter

The perimeter indicates the total distance around a geometric figure.

∴ A rectangle with four sides, a, b, c, and d, has a perimeter a+b+c+d.

Since two of its opposite sides measure the same, the perimeter of a rectangle = 2l+2b, where l= length and w=width.

Perimeter of a rectangle = 2l+2w

Perimeter of a square with four equal sides = 4l (length).

Perimeter of a triangle with sides a, b, and c, is = a+b+c.

Perimeter trapezoid is the sum of its sides a, b, c, d.

A paralleogram has 2 opposite sides that are equal in length.

∴ Its perimeter is 2l + 2w where l+length and w= width.

Circumference

The circumference of a circle is given by the formula $2\pi r$, where π is a constant of value 3.14 and r is the radius of the circle.

Since the diameter of a circle is 2r, we may say that the circle's circumference is = πd.

Area

The difference between perimeter and area is that the former measures the distance covered by the borders to enclose a space. In contrast, the area measures the space enclosed by the borders, as mentioned earlier. For example, if the fence is the border, the grass cover inside the fence is the area.

Grid Method

We can measure the area simply using the grid method.

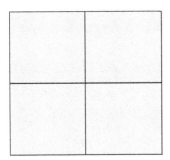

In this method, you calculate the number of grids, 4. You need to know the measurements of each square of the grid. Supposing each square is two cm in length and width, the size of each square will be 4cm^2.

Since there are 4 such squares, the total area = 16cm^2

If the area enclosed by the grid is not an exact square, then it becomes more challenging to find the area.

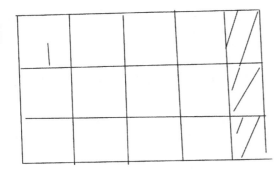

In the grid above, the boxes marked with slants are not squares, but fractions of them. Calculate the number of full squares, 12.

The area of each square with length 1cm and width 1cm is 1cm^2.

The area of 12 full squares is 12cm².

The half squares are three. This is of the same size as 1.5 squares of area 1.5cm².

Add them to get 13.5 squares. The area of this grid is 13.5cm² assuming the squares have each an area of 1cm²

In real life, we don't always get the grid layout, and we need formulas to calculate the area of a geometric space.

Applying Formulae

i) Area of a rectangle = Height ✕ Width
ii) Area of a square = Length²
iii) Area of a triangle = ½ ✕ base ✕ height

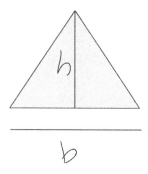

The perpendicular line drawn measures the height of the triangle, and b is the base (*isu. edu/media/library/student, n.d.*)

iv) Area of a parallelogram is b ✕ h, where b= base and h = height

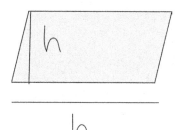

v) Area of trapezoid is ½ (b1+b2) ✕ h, where b1= base 1, and b2 = base 2.

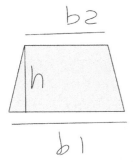

vi) Area of a circle =π r²

Problems:

i) Find the area of A.

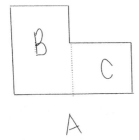

What will be the area of space A?

You will need to draw an imaginary line through A to mark out two manageable areas: a rectangle B and a square C. You can now easily find the areas of B and C and add them to get the total area of A.

You can split the entire area into as many rectangles and squares as you can to find the area.

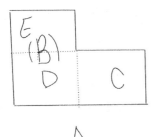

In this picture, I have divided area B into two smaller squares, E and D.

ii) Find the area of the path (P) around the garden (G).

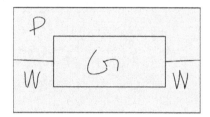

The fastest way to solve this problem is by finding the total area (P+G) and the area of the garden (G). You can subtract them to get the area of the path (*skillsyouneed. com, n.d.*).

For example, the width of the outer border is 12 cm, and the length is 10 cm. The Area of P+G = 120cm².

If the width of the path (w) is 2 cm, then its total width (both sides) is 4 cm. This means the middle rectangle or G is 16–4=12cm.

Similarly, you need to subtract 4 cm from the height of the whole area (P+G) to get the height of the inner rectangle G = 10–4=6.

The area of G is W×H = 72cm².

The area of the path is 120–72= 48cm²

Volume

i) Volume of a cube

A cube has six identical square faces, if we consider each side of the square as 's' the volume of a cube $V = s^3$

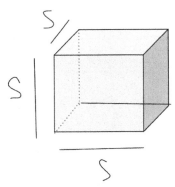

If s= 3cm, V= 3 × 3 × 3 = 9cm³

ii) Area of a rectangular prism:

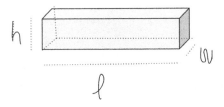

h = height, w = width, and l= length of a rectangular prism, then its volume V =l × b × w.

Suppose the corresponding values are 4″, 2″, and 8″. In that case, the volume V of the rectangular prism is 64inch³

iii) Volume of a cylinder:

If r = radius, and the height is h, then volume V of a cylinder is $\pi r^2 h$. You may remember that πr^2 = area of the circle. And h = height.

You may also remember that the circumference of a circle is $2\pi r$, where 2π is the diameter of a circle. So, you may find out the volume of a cylinder when these values are given by substituting them in the formula.

iii) Volume of a sphere:

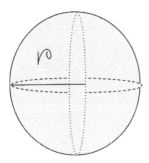

$4/3\ \pi r^3$, where r=radius.

iv) Volume of a cone of height h, and radius r = $\frac{1}{3}\ \pi r^2 h$.

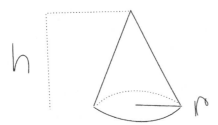

v) Volume of a pyramid of base b and height h is = $\frac{1}{3}$ bh.

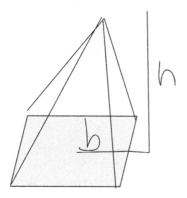

Charts And Graphs

Bar Graphs

These are pictorial descriptions of different data using bars of different heights. A bar graph will have two axes; a vertical and a horizontal. The values can be put against the axes to show the comparison of data.

If you have 'categories' of data, bar graphs are useful; for continuous data like showing the weights of a person, we use a histogram.

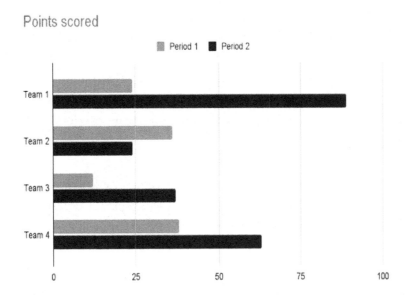

Line Graphs

Line graphs, or line charts, show a series of data points connected by a straight line. It represents changes in values over time. These graphs are useful to determine the relationship between two values of interdependent data sets. Because of their nature, line graphs have a predictability value.

The most important observation is the **slope of the line** drawn. Depending on how steep it is, it can compare the magnitude of change between two consecutive points on the graph.

Line graphs have a horizontal x-axis and a vertical y-axis. Usually the line graphs represent positive number values. Hence the axes intersect near the bottom of the y-axis and at the left end of the x-axis. The point where the axes intersect is (0,0).

You have to plot categories of data on each axis. For example, the x-axis can have days, months, or years. You can plot money you made in dollars against this data. You have to plot the data points and connect them by a line in a dot to dot pattern.

A line graph has following components:

- Title: The title informs us about the graph.
- Labels: The horizontal and the vertical labels inform what kinds of data are depicted.
- Scales: The horizontal and the vertical scales inform the quantity of the data.
- Points: Points or dots on the graph manifest (x,y) coordinates or ordered pairs. You can plot multiple data lines in a line graph. The data on the **x-axis** is **independent variable** and those on the **y-axis** is **dependent variable**.
- Lines: Lines are the straight lines connecting the points that give estimated values between the points.

The two axes must follow the same scales. Plot data on the x-axis that do not depend on anything like time. Plot changeable data along the y-axis. The resultant straight line always progresses horizontally, with a unique value of y for each point on the x-axis.

To read a line graph, you need to do the following.

- Study the title.
- Observe the labels on the axes.
- Study the patterns coming out to follow the course.
- Look at the data values for exact figures.

It is called a line graph because a straight line joins the data. The x-axis shows texts, and does not handle mathematical data; the y-axis can show numbers. The graph represents a continuous flow of data over a time period against a more general scale (*cuemath. com, n.d.*).

Pie Charts

Pie charts record data in a circular pattern. This is further divided into sections that represent a portion of a part of the total.

The total value of the pie is 100%. It is a circle that subtends an angle of 360°.

$\therefore$ The whole pie= 360°

Formulae to calculate the pie

If you have to calculate the percentage of the given data, use the following formula.

- (Frequency / Total frequency) *100.

In order to change into degrees, use the formula:

- (Data Given / Total value of data)*360°

You may use the following steps to find out the percentage for a given pie chart.

- Grade the given data and calculate the total data.
- Divide the different grades
- Convert the data obtained into percentages
- Calculate the degrees.

Example: Money spent at a shop by Mary is indicated by a pie chart. The total value of the data is 10 and the amount spent on each category is interpreted as follows:

- Ice Cream - 2
- Candies - 4
- Cupcake- 1
- Chocolates - 3

Applying the formula: (Frequency ÷ Total Frequency) × 100, we can convert the data into percentage values for each item as follows.

Amount spent on chocolates: (3/10)× 100 = 30%
Amount spent on candies: (4/10)× 100 = 40%
Amount spent on the cupcake: (1/10)× 100 = 10%
Amount spent on ice cream: (2/10)× 100 = 20%

Chapter Three Summary and Key Takeaways: Mathematics Study Guide

This study guide was devoted to helping you further develop your math skills and understanding of numbers. Here are the key points we've discussed in this section.

- Numbers
- Basic Math Functions
- Fractions
- Order of Operations
- Algebra
- Geometry
- Inequalities
- Measurements
- Charts and Graphs
- Math Strategies

Thus far we have covered reading, writing, and math skills. It is time to put your knowledge to the test in the second part of the book; Practice Tests.

Part 2- Practice Tests

How to Use These Practice Tests

The following are three practice tests based on each of the previous study guides. Each test is divided into three sections, each focusing on a different skill. This is meant to mirror the format of the actual exam.

You can time yourself or go through the questions at your own pace.

Don't forget; Your reading and writing skills will come into play in all three sections of the exam!

NOTE: The formal exam is timed. It is suggested that you time yourself for some of the practice tests. See the appendix to find specifics of the exam.

Practice Test #1

Reading

Fact And Opinion

1. What is the closest word related to 'fact?'

   A. Feel
   B. Think
   C. Sometimes
   D. Definitely

2. There are some words below. Choose if they match the definition for 'fact' or 'opinion.'

   A. Not: i) Fact ii) opinion
   B. Happened: i) Fact ii) opinion
   C. Should: i) Fact ii) opinion
   D. Safely: i) Fact ii) opinion

3. Choose which of the answers match with the definition of **fact**

   A. should
   B. intelligent

    C. my sense is

    D. took place on

    E. in the past

        Ans.1: A and E

        Ans. 2: B and C

        Ans. 3: D and E

        Ans. 4: None of the above

4. State if the words given below are true or false for 'opinion.' Please insert a tick in the relevant box (not shown in the text).

    i. might: True / False

    ii. happened: True / False

    iii. expect: True / False

    iv. At all times: True / False

    v. best: True / False

    vi. intelligence: True / False

    vii. will: True / False

5. Choose matching definitions for the terms: "fact"/ "opinion."

    i. Generally: Fact/Opinion

    ii. Could: Fact/Opinion

    iii. Conceivably: Fact/Opinion

    iv. Guardedly: Fact/Opinion

    v. His sense is: Fact/Opinion

    vi. Verified: Fact/Opinion

    vii. My point of view: Fact/Opinion

    viii. Proved: Fact/Opinion

Which of The Following

6. Which of the following is not the flavor of spice?

    A. bitter

    B. salty

    C. sour

    D. sweet

    E. umami

    F. basil

7. Entries in outlines are generally arranged according to which of the following relationships of ideas?

    A. Verbatim and deductive

    B. Concrete and abstract

    C. Linear and recurring

    D. Main and subordinate

8. A teacher wrote two samples on the blackboard from the student's samples. He demonstrated to the students the proper technique for proofreading. He then asked the students to do their proofreading from their own writing samples.

    Which of the following methods is the teacher's purpose?

    A. Ideas

    B. Organization

    C. Voice

    D. Convention

In the following questions, you will find a question or questions after each statement or passage based on the text. After reading the statement or passage, choose the best answer to each question from among the given choices. Answer all questions following a statement or passage based on the text's stated or implied meaning. You may not have any previous knowledge of the topics related to the statements and passages. Try to answer every question.

9. As a pioneer filmmaker, Marguerite Dura's achievement in filmmaking was marked by a refusal to become a professional in the cinema, which implies prestige, influence, financial backing, and even know-how. Although she made many films, she admitted to knowing very little about the technology of cinema. She said she had no reason to learn anymore: "I want to remain where I am, on the first grounds of cinema, in the primitive zones."

   The passage is mainly concerned with

   A. upbraiding critics' failure to recognize the work of a particular filmmaker
   B. expressing the attitude of a particular filmmaker
   C. evaluating the style of a particular filmmaker
   D. criticizing the technical deficiencies of a particular filmmaker
   E. deliberating the gist of the works of a particular filmmaker.

Read the following paragraph and then answer the next question.

One promising energy source is a sophisticated version of the basic windmills that could grind grain, drain the land, and pump water for centuries.

Coupled with modern storage batteries, very large windmills can also satisfy total energy needs for rural areas, towns, and even small cities, particularly in localities with strong and prevalent winds.

Wind power has many advantages. First, no new technology is required. Second, the energy source is unlimited and one hundred percent clean. Third, one can install or operate windmills with relatively little capital investment. But wind power has significant disadvantages, too.

Most obviously, it only works in a small number of places. Less evidently, putting up a lot of big windmills might change the weather and environment in ways that no one intended. Woodlands of big windmills could become uncomfortable to look at. Lastly, the amount of power that could be made with wind energy would not be enough to meet the country's major power requirements.

However, a network of sea-based windmills that are placed on deep-ocean buoys and driven by the same winds that once powered sailing vessels all over the world could generate a substantial fraction of the world's electrical energy—especially if the buoy-based windmills could be linked to land by superconducting power transmission cables that are loss-free.

10. The passage states that sea-based windmills could be an efficient source of energy actively if:

   A. One could build them in shallow water.
   B. They were located near significant urban ports.
   C. They were constructed on stationary platforms.
   D. The power they produced could be transferred efficiently to shore.
   E. One could store the power they produced in advanced high-capacity batteries.

11. Which of the following best describes the construction of the passage?

   A. A series of interrelated events arranged chronologically.
   B. A controversial theory is proposed and then convincingly defended.
   C. An unforeseen problem is described, and diverse examples are cited.
   D. A criticism is conveyed, evaluated, and then ignored.
   E. A problematical issue is discussed, and an incomplete solution is discussed.

Questions #12, #13, and #14 refer to the lines 5, 10, 15, 20, 25, and 30 of the following two passages.

Passage 1

When managed properly, ecotourism— responsible travel to natural areas conserving the (line5) environment and sustaining the well-being of indigenous people—is less harmful than many other environmental uses. One can manage the influences of ecotourism to realize a balance between preservation and progress; such balance can be obtained, for instance, by restricting both (line 10) the scale and number of tours in a particular area and by including environmentally-conscious meals, lodging, waste management, and wildlife viewing rules into the tours. Further, ecotourism can encourage local caretaking of natural resources, habitats, and wildlife (line 15) by fostering economic incentives for underprivileged villages or communities.

Passage 2

(line 20) The environmental consequences of the Lapa Rios Eco Lodge in Costa Rica are undisputed. First, the LR nature reserve and its adjoining forests have demonstrated remarkable re-forestation and growth of vegetation since the commencing of ecotourism in the area in the 1990s. (line 25) Second, the increasing population of tourists at LR has not led to negative impacts for the company planned for such happenings from the start: trails were constructed to handle several synchronous tours with a scattering of the crowd, and the trail policy strictly restricts the (line 30) number of excursions per day per trail (two) and tourists per tour (eight).

12. The authors of the passages agree that:

   A. Preservation is more consequential than progress.
   B. Measuring the success of ecotourism may be challenging
   C. Ecotourism is understandably costlier than regular tourism
   D. Positive impacts can be obtainable from ecotourism when done properly
   E. Responsibility for monitoring the environment is up to the local people

13. Which of the following statements best states the relationship between the two passages?

   A. Passage 1 narrates the causes of an event, and Passage 2 concentrates on the effects of the event.
   B. Passage 1 states current policies, but Passage 2 proposes future policies.
   C. Passage 1 makes a general argument, but Passage 2 makes a specific argument.
   D. Passage 1 presents a problem for which a speculative solution is given in Passage 2.
   E. Passage 1 makes a claim challenged with a counterclaim in Passage 2.

14. As against the author of Passage 2, the author of Passage 1 said about

   A. the number of tours allowed.
   B. the casual impacts of ecotourism.
   C. the economic influence on local people.
   D. the ecological aftereffects of ecotourism.
   E. The endorsed modes of travel through natural reserves.

Study the following reading material and then answer questions # 15, #16, 17, #18, and #19.

Yellow Springs has seen a major decline in minor crime rates over the last 5 years. Officials give credence to the "after-school programs" for this extraordinary achievement. The real credit goes to the mayor, who implemented, along with the officials, many new projects to engage the teenagers after school hours.

This happened after the police found out that the teenagers committed many petty crimes during afternoon hours. The officials suggested various after-school programs to the school boards and requested them to increase their numbers. Police officers, school officials, and community members volunteered their time and skills to produce art, music, dance, and mentoring programs at the local high schools. Now students are more busy exploring their creative sides in more compelling ways. They spend quality time after school instead of loitering the streets in the afternoons. The rates of graffiti declined by more than 50%, arrests for shoplifting were less than before, and vandalism was less reported.

Undoubtedly Yellow Springs saw many benefits from these programs that were easy to implement. The crime rates declined, but there was also a positive upsurge in community feeling.

More and more young people volunteer their time in the community, and older teens act as mentors and guides to younger students. Yellow springs is now growing stronger. It is now a model for other communities who hope to bring about such changes.

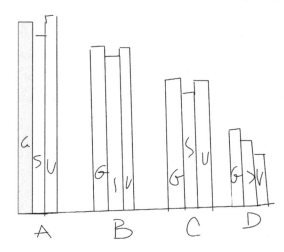

Supposing A = 2013, B = 2014, C = 2015, and D = 2016 to show the petty crime rates, and G=graffiti, S= shoplifting, and V=vandalism, answer the following question.

15. According to the bar chart, the first year the vandalism rates were less than shop-lifting rates was:

    A. 2013
    B. 2104
    C. 2015
    D. 2016

16. The main objective of the paragraph mentioned above is to:

    A. Persuade the public that art and entertainment programs must be better funded.
    B. Generate awareness that after-school programs help reduce teen crime rates.
    C. Persuade the people that after-school programs for the teens benefit them by guaranteeing that they stay away from trouble.
    D. Clarify the effects of after-school programs on crime rates in Yellow Springs.

17. According to the bar chart, the biggest petty crime rate in 2015 was

    A. Shoplifting
    B. Vandalism
    C. Graffiti
    D. None of the above

18. The benefits of the after-school program in the paragraph include all except:

    A. An increase in community awareness.
    B. Decline in crime rates
    C. Students mentoring the juniors
    D. Petty crime rates by teens increased in 2016.

19. The paragraph mentions that the success of the program was due to:

    A. Willingness of the townspeople to provide whatever expenditure was necessary to make the program work.
    B. The police suggested that those who would cooperate with the program would be excused from paying fines.
    C. People volunteered their time and talents to make the program successful.

D. The students stated their interest in participating in after-school programs to keep them busy with some productive work.

Read the following passage before you answer the questions numbers #20, #21, #22, #23, and #24.

School dropout rates continue to trouble policymakers, school districts, and responsible citizens. Many students who dropped out before graduation claimed they had to take recourse to this action to earn money to support their families and help to pay bills. This is pertinent because the high unemployment rate and scarcity of jobs make it seem that everyone has to contribute whatever they can to run the household in the current scenario. One method to address this problem is to pay the students for school attendance.

Parents tell their ward that it is their 'job' to attend school when they grumble and grouse about attending school. Students are <u>responsible</u> for attending school, and the parents' responsibility is to go to work. However, the parents are paid for job attendance while students receive no monetary compensation for attending school. Will paying the students to attend school decrease school dropout rates?

The advocates of this theory say yes. Paying the students alleviates the necessity to work a minimum wage to contribute to the household bills. This effectively reduces school dropouts. With fewer dropouts, more and more individuals will earn their diplomas. They will be better prepared to attend universities or trade schools to pursue further education and land better job prospects. Paying students for school attendance is an excellent idea, and school districts should give it a thought.

20. Which of the following from the paragraph is an example of 'opinion?'

A. The rates of dropouts among high school students <u>is</u> a continuing worry for school districts, policymakers, and responsible citizens.
B. A great idea is to reward the students with pay packages for going to school, and school districts should consider it seriously.
C. While the children get no monetary compensation for school attendance, their parents get paid for going to work.
D. This is pertinent because many students drop out of school before graduation to work to support their families and help them to pay the bills.

21. The word <u>responsible</u> highlighted in the text most closely means

   A. At fault
   B. Executive
   C. Obedient
   D. Concerned

22. The 'main idea' of the passage is:

   A. When encumbered with a lot of taxes, it is challenging to take good care of the household.
   B. Motivating the students to stay longer in the school produces better-educated individuals.
   C. It is increasingly burdensome for families to earn a living wage
   D. One of the ideas to help the dropout rates is to pay the students for school attendance.

23. For a 'persuasive text,' the passage lacks:

   A. A counterargument
   B. A conclusive paragraph
   C. A thesis statement
   D. Supporting evidence

24. The appropriate graphic representation for the passage would be:

   A. A bar graph depicting the rates of poverty in American families
   B. A pie chart showing what the most popular majors the high school students are interested in.
   C. A pie chart showing the number of students entering college, joining the military services, or entering immediately into the workforce.
   D. A bar graph that shows the dropout rates in the last ten years.

Read the following paragraph and answer Question numbers #25 and #26.

Dolphins make two principal kinds of vocalizations. They are clicks and whistles. They reserve clicks for echolocation and whistles for communication with others. Dolphins make the Clicks in rapid succession, echoing back to them. These broadband bursts help them with information related to their surroundings. Whistles are sent in narrow-band signals. The dolphins whistle to identify and call each other. Researchers have found that large schools of dolphins use a highly developed mode of intercommunication while threatened by predators like sharks. In the face of an unanticipated threat, a group of dolphins moves in near-unison to prevent the threat. Thus, they rely on both visual and auditory signals to transmit their location and interpret the location of others in the pod.

25. Which of the following answers support the concept "Researchers study the communication system in dolphins because it gives a knowledge of an animal's intelligence level" of the passage best?

    A. Dolphins make two principal kinds of vocalizations; they are clicks and whistles.
    B. Clicks are made in rapid succession that echo back to them. These broadband bursts help them with information related to their surroundings.
    C. Whistles are sent in narrow-band signals.
    D. A group of dolphins, in the face of an unanticipated threat, move in near unison to prevent the threat. Thus, they rely on both visual and auditory signals to transmit their location and interpret the location of others in the pod.

26. Which of the following is the "main idea" of the passage?

    A. Showing the readers how dolphins differ from other sea animals.
    B. To convince the readers to be kind toward dolphins and help protect them.
    C. To tell the readers about the different strategies by which the dolphins communicate.
    D. To regale the readers with stories about how dolphins are similar to humans.

27. Which of the following is more likely to mean "vocalization?"

    A. Oral sounds
    B. Clicks
    C. Meaningful sounds
    D. Music

28. *Mahatama Gandhi took charge of the Indian National Congress in 1921. It consisted of a group of thirteen men who fought against discrimination and unfair taxation meted out to the farmers and city laborers by the British Government ruling in India then.*

   Gandhi and his followers used the tactic of non-violence as a means of civil disobedience to resist British domination over the life of the common Indian people. Non-violence meant not obeying unfair and discriminatory laws and policies by adopting peaceful noncooperation with the British government.

   The British retaliated to this resistance with a strengthened military force that often caused the loss of human lives. Gandhi was imprisoned in 1942 for his "radical" ideas. Even then, he refused to acknowledge violence as an option to fight the British presence on the Indian subcontinent. Gandhi gained international acclamation for his "hunger strikes" when he refused to eat until the British changed their unjust policies.

   The orderly arrangement of the paragraph above is an example of

   A. Chronological order
   B. Spatial order
   C. Descending order of importance
   D. Ascending order of importance

Read the following passage and answer Questions #29- #30.

Stories can be of many kinds. The most difficult of any kind of story is telling a humorous story. Humorous is American; the British name such stories comic stories while the French call them witty. But there is a more subtle difference between a humorous story and a comic one. Humorous storytelling is mostly about how the story is told. A comic story, on the other hand, tells us about the matter.

29. What is the main purpose of this passage?

   A. Entertain the reader about something
   B. Engage the reader about something
   C. Motivate the reader about something
   D. Explain to the reader about something

30. What do you think the author is mainly implying in the passage?

    A. Humorous stories are most engaging.
    B. Humorous stories are difficult to write
    C. Humorous stories are British.
    D. Humorous stories write about funny things.

Read the following passage and then answer questions #31- #33.

A humorous story can be lengthy; take a much more circuitous route and <u>get nowhere.</u> The comic and witty stories, on the other hand, should be brief and have a definite end. It seems to a reader that while the humorous stories gently bubble, the comic and witty stories erupt with mirth. It may be safe to conclude that a humorous story is truly a work of art, and only artists can tell them. No such talent is required to narrate a comic or witty story. A humorous story is native to America and is narrated gravely. The storyteller makes serious attempts to hide the story's nature, making the story's essence more subtle. On the other hand, a comic story announces the funny nature of the story at its beginning. They prove their point as soon as possible.

31. What do you think the author believes about humorous storytellers?

    A. They are very serious and grave people
    B. They are more skilled than comic writers.
    C. They are not to be believed.
    D. They use greater flair and mastery to evoke laughter from the readers than comic storytellers.

32. Which of the following options best describes how the author organized the main argument?

    A. They compared and contrasted the different story types and then gave proper examples.
    B. They identified a distinct storytelling style and then discussed the merits of one over the other's weaknesses.
    C. The authors cleverly did not take a side and delicately suggested the custom of humorous storytelling to show its excellence over comic stories.
    D. The authors gave a cultural distinction between humorous storytelling and then gave an inventory of the contributions of each class to the art of storytelling.

33. What do you think the underlined term "get nowhere" from the passage means?

    A. The story remains unfinished, and it's up to the reader to finish it.
    B. The story is dense and witless.
    C. The story may arrive at no obvious conclusion.
    D. The storyteller does not know how to finish the story.

34. **Read the following passage and then answer question #34**

    We may be tempted to think that our eyes are like mirrors reflecting what is in front of us. Researchers showed that the brain constantly creates the impression of an uninterrupted surrounding. In the last five minutes, you blinked a hundred times. There were interruptions in the visual world of which you were unaware. Probably you have not noticed that you have a nose. It is really your brain that filters it out of your visual field. You are unaware of the artery that runs through the retina's center. It creates a blind spot in your visual field, and you never notice the hole the optic nerve leaves. You can see the blind spot by covering your left eye with your hand. Look at O on the left with your right eye. Move your head closer to O; the X will vanish as it enters the blind spot.

    O   X

    What is the main purpose of the passage?

    A. To convince the readers to pay attention to the blind spot.
    B. To narrate how visual perception occurs.
    C. One should be concerned if O and X vanish.
    D. Vision is a passive process.

Writing

1. Which sentence is in "passive voice?"

    A. Sammy will not be at the concert because he has hurt his leg.
    B. The poem was written by Shelly.
    C. The girls decided to go to a movie.
    D. Clyde covered the distance in five minutes.

2. Which sentence has the complete predicate underlined?

    A. Danny's pet was soaked and grimy after the boy's hike <u>to the park</u>.
    B. <u>Fifteen cars</u> raced across the mountain path.
    C. Although she could not recognize the man by sight, <u>Sarah identified her attacker's voice</u>.
    D. The man <u>walked along the side of the pavement</u>.

3. Which punctuation mark will you use to fill in the blank of the sentence?

    "It is raining ___ I should carry an umbrella."

    A. A comma.
    B. A dash
    C. A full stop.
    D. A colon.

4. What part of speech is the underlined word?

    The cat ran <u>up</u> the wall.

    A. Verb
    B. Conjunction
    C. Adverb
    D. Preposition

5. Which sentence has an error in spelling?

    A. Don't feel embarrassed because you tripped and fell in front of the entire class.
    B. I have applied for admission to the college.
    C. Unfortunately, Sarah is not with us here due to unavoidable circumstances.
    D. Apparently, he is not well-heeled.

6. Which sentence has an incorrect capitalization?

    A. Mom asked, "Did you do your homework?"
    B. We will go to visit NASA in July.
    C. Martha and uncle Sam went to the same college, the University of Denver.

D. Maria and her sister Gloria performed the dances.

7. Which sentence has not used the correct apostrophe?

   A. The fox caught it's foot in the trap.
   B. We couldn't go to school today.
   C. It's Marie's birthday.
   D. This is our parents' car.

8. The error in this sentence is?

   "Mary is going on his road trip next month."

   A. Error in verb tense.
   B. No error
   C. Error in pronoun-antecedent agreement.
   D. Error in subject-verb agreement.

9. Which answer correctly capitalizes the title of the book: over the bridges and through the forests: an excursion to grandmother's place

   A. Over the bridges and Through the forests: an excursion to grandmother's place.
   B. Over the Bridges and Through the forests: an Excursion to Grandmother's place.
   C. Over the Bridges and Through the Forests: an Excursion to Grandmother's Place.
   D. Over The Bridges And Through The Forests: An Excursion To Grandmother's Place.

10. Which sentence shows the correct word choice?

    A. Laura did not except my greetings.
    B. There are too many sand particles on the beach to count.
    C. Whether you win or loose, you must give your best shot.
    D. Robbie likes playing basketball more then playing soccer.

11. Which of the following sentences tells about the stage of the writing process where students appraise the content of their writing before concentrating on grammatical or spelling mistakes?

    A. Revising

B. Editing
C. Prewriting
D. Publishing

12. The purpose for writing is all of these except:

A. To delight
B. To inform
C. To convince
D. To impress

13. A writing structure that follows a story with a beginning, a middle, and an end is called a:

A. Persuasive writing
B. Descriptive writing
C. Narrative writing
D. Argumentative writing

14. A writer should know their audience. "Knowing the audience" means:

A. Meeting the audience ahead of writing to inform them about the background of the text and answer the queries they may have on the subject.
B. Knowing who the readers are and adapting the text's diction, syntax, and organization, keeping the reader's tastes, interests, and understanding in mind.
C. Understanding the topic correctly to present a text acceptable to all and sundry.
D. Writing about exciting events and people.

15. While checking an online source, you should ask all of these questions except

A. Have I heard of this publication or is it linked to an organization I am aware of?
B. What are the author's credentials that make them suitable for this kind of work?
C. Do I consider the author is right?
D. Is the information an unbiased and objective presentation?

16. A student is writing about ancient civilizations' migration patterns. They would need as a reference:

    A. A Dictionary
    B. A Thesaurus
    C. A primary document source
    D. An atlas

17. If you are in the editing phase of writing, then as a paraprofessional, the most pertinent task would be:

    A. Amend the inconsistent parts of the text for the student.
    B. Motivate the student to go through their texts as many times as necessary to sort out the inconsistencies and mistakes and correct them.
    C. Ask key questions that will help the student identify their mistakes.
    D. You will proofread and do all the corrections to save any more trouble.

18. Identify the sentence with a "misplaced modifier?"

    A. Only after all the students have come will we know who is absent.
    B. James mentioned Tracy could come with him for a ride in the text.
    C. According to the police officers, the cause of the fire was accidental.
    D. The yellow car left paint transfer on the blue car following the collision.

19. When you have a word in mind but cannot recall it, you will use:

    A. An Atlas
    B. A Dictionary
    C. A Directory
    D. A Thesaurus

20. <u>How many times must</u> I tell <u>you</u>. <u>Do not leave the kitchen</u> <u>with the stove still on</u>!

    Which part of the abovementioned expression is wrong?

    A. How many times must I
    B. you.
    C. Do not leave the kitchen

D. With the stove still on!

21. Lisa allowed the older woman behind her move first because she had less items in her cart than Lisa.

Which of the underlined sections of the sentence above are wrong?

A. Lisa allowed, than Lisa.
B. her move first, than Lisa
C. Had less
D. her move first and had less

22. Find out the adverb:

Suzy unthinkingly grabbed for her yellow dress and tore it off at the seams.

A. Grabbed
B. Unthinkingly
C. Yellow
D. off

23. Identify the misspelled word:

A. Salivery
B. Desperate
C. Management
D. Excursion

24. Identify the predicate of the sentence: Sam and his mother went to the supermarket.

A. Sam and his mother
B. went to the supermarket
C. Sam and his mother went
D. to the supermarket

25. **In the sentences below, a part has been underlined. Do you think the underlined portions are correct? If not, then how should they be revised? Choose from the correct options:**

i) Police personnel and firefighters risk their lives; <u>therefore</u>, professionals like doctors and lawyers have similar important influences on our lives medically and legally.

A. Therefore is correct choice
B. But
C. Nevertheless
D. And

ii) Sports are a very significant part of our lives, as was shown in 2006 when billions of people assembled to get involved with the <u>World Cup either through playing, watching, or advertising.</u>

A. World cup either through playing, through watching, or through advertising.
B. World cup either through playing, watching, or advertising.
C. World cup either through playing, watching, or through advertising.
D. world cup either through playing, watching, or advertising.
E. World cup either through playing, watching, or advertising for it.

iii) During the <u>summer, many students go to summer camps that teach skills about fellowship, diligence, and honesty.</u>

A. summer, many students go to summer camps that teach them skills about fellowship, diligence, and honesty
B. summer, many students go to camps that teach skills about fellowship, diligence, and honesty.
C. summer, many students go to summer camps that teach skills about fellowship, diligence, and following honesty
D. Summer, many students go to camps that teach skills about fellowship, diligence, and honesty.

iv) Learning new skills can be challenging <u>after one reaches a particular age.</u>

A. After one reaches a particular age
B. After they reaches a particular age

C. After they reach a particular age

D. After we reach a particular age

v) <u>For buildings in typically hotter climatic regions</u>, it is rather important to have good ventilation.

A. For buildings in typically hotter climatic regions,

B. For someone in buildings in typically hotter climatic regions,

C. For buildings in typically hot climatic regions,

D. Buildings in typically hotter climatic regions,

26. In the next three questions, choose which option would use a comma correctly.

i) "The girl in red," whispered Laura "is the new girl."

A. girl, in the

B. whispered Laura,

C. new, girl

D. No error

ii) Oh she forgot to bring her homework.

A. Oh,

B. she forgot,

C. to bring,

D. No error

iii) The alligator, a water animal sometimes comes to the land.

A. sometimes,

B. water animal,

C. No error

D. comes to,

27. Choose the correct option:

I often have difficulty remembering which is which, affect ("to alter" or "to impact") and effect ("to bring about" or to achieve)."

A. "to achieve)."

B. "to achieve")

C. "to achieve).

D. to achieve.

28. Which is the correct verb form for the following sentence:

    A. Ever since he was a child, he has wanted to go to Africa.
    B. Ever since he was a child, he will want to go to Africa.
    C. Ever since he was a child, he is wanting to go to Africa.
    D. Ever since he was a child, he was wanting to go to Africa.

29. Once she was motivated, she did it perfect again.

    A. did perfectly
    B. was perfectly
    C. could perfectly
    D. No error

30. Identify the correct verb form:

    A. They will have finished their dinner before she has reached the house.
    B. They will have finished their dinner before she reaches the house.
    C. They will have finished their dinner before she will have reached the house.
    D. They will have finished their dinner before she is reaching the house.

31. Which is the verb in the following sentence?

    The weather changes affected the crops in the winter season.

    A. Crops
    B. Changes
    C. Affected
    D. In

32. Identify the correct form of the sentence: "I would have given it to you if you <u>would have asked me</u>.

    A. would ask
    B. could ask
    C. had asked
    D. would have asked me.

33. Pick the correct option for the marked part of the sentence from the choices given below.

    i) <u>The committee, as a whole, are united</u> against the new regulation by the chairman.

    A. The committee, as a whole, are united
    B. The committee, as a whole, is united,
    C. As a whole the committee are united
    D. The committee are united as a whole.

    ii) Anyone on the boy's soccer team <u>was invited to put their name</u> on the Varsity team.

    A. was invited to put their name
    B. was invited to put his name
    C. is invited to put their name
    D. puts their name by invitation

    iii) <u>Each of us have their own</u> method of analyzing a situation.

    A. Each of us have their own
    B. Each of us has their own
    C. Each have our own way
    D. Each of us has our own

34.

    i) Choose the appropriate word combinations to fill the gaps of the sentence below.

    The — the author used to describe an accident was so nebulous that the readers at first glance found it —

A. puzzle, practical
B. euphemism, incoherent
C. edification, circumspect
D. potentate, didactic

ii) The musician evoked powerful emotions. Evoke means:

A. Cried
B. Sang
C. Clapped
D. Induced

iii) The musician played the lyre. A lyre is a:

A. String instrument of the harp class
B. Percussion instrument
C. Wind instrument
D. Reed type instrument.

Math

1. The teacher draws a square. He then turns to his students and asks if this square is made up of square units, what will be the square root of the square?

    A. It should be exactly half the total number of unit squares that make the big square.
    B. The sum total of unit squares within the big square.
    C. Only the number of unit squares that make the perimeter of the square.
    D. The number of unit squares that make a side.

2. A tank of water is 70% full. How much of it is empty?

    A. 70%
    B. 3/7
    C. 3/10
    D. 30/1

3. Which one of the following is in order from least to greatest?

   A. 5/2, 0.25, 9/50, -8, -7⅘ , -¾
   B. -7⅘ , -¾, 9/50, -8, 0.25, 5/2
   C. -8, -7⅘ , -¾, 9/50, 0.25, 5/2
   D. 0.25, 9/50, -¾, -8, -7⅘ , 5/2

4. What is the digit in the thousandth place in the number 3,243.7658?

   A. 2
   B. 5
   C. 6
   D. 3

5. Which one represents 40% of 80?

   A. 32
   B. 60
   C. 50
   D. 20

6. You are asked to multiply two numbers, 550.4 and 20.496. Which of the following represents the approximate value?

   A. 110,000
   B. 11,000
   C. 12,500
   D. 115,000

7. Find the area of the triangle of sides 12 inches, 10 inches, and 10 inches in the picture below.

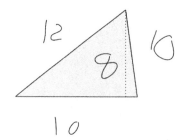

A. 30 square inches
B. 120 square inches
C. 40 square inches
D. 80 square inches

8. Derive the equation given below to find the value for x.

    $[(84)^2 \div 28 \times 12] \div 24 = 7 \times x$

    A. the value of x=20
    B. x=18
    C. x=54
    D. 32

9. Solve the equation given below to find the value of x.

    $-224 + (-314) \times (-9) = x$

    A. -547
    B. 547
    C. -2602
    D. 2602

10. Find the value of $(6-2)^2 + 15 \div 5$

    A. 13
    B. 18
    C. 19
    D. 21

11. Solve the equation given below.

    $-4x = 16$

    A. 4
    B. -4
    C. 64
    D. 20

12. Find the mean value of the data set {–4, 0, 4, 8, 12, 16}

    A. 44
    B. –40
    C. 20
    D. 6

13. Find the missing number in the sequence: 9, 4, –1, —, –11

    A. –4
    B. –6
    C. –5
    D. –9

14. In the graph that has been drawn for you, can you find the coordinates for the point P ?

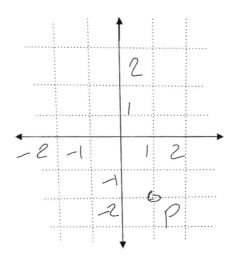

    A. (1, 2)
    B. (1, -2)
    C. (-1, -2)
    D. (2, -1)

15. If, in this graph, the x-coordinate represents the time in months, and the y-co-ordinate represents the number of books Martha read, then, provided that she continues the trend throughout, how many books will Martha have completed by the 7th month?

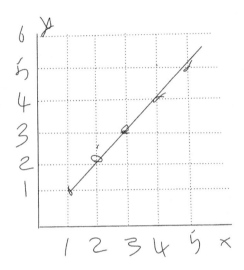

    A. 5.5 books
    B. 6 books
    C. 7 books
    D. Not known.

16. Find the volume of the rectangular prism with a length 8 inches, width 2 inches, and height 2 inches.

    A. 32 cubic inches
    B. 12 inches
    C. 12 cubic inches
    D. 32 inches

17. You as a paraprofessional find that a student has written this number sentence to describe a mathematical condition, "The difference of 5 and 2 is to be multiplied by the sum of 2 and 4."

    This is what the student wrote: (5–2)*2+4

Do you think that the student wrote it correctly? If not, then what, according to you, should be the correct expression of the equation?

A. 5–2*2+4
B. The student wrote it correctly, and no further change is necessary.
C. 5–2*(2+4)
D. (5–2)*(2+4)

18. The diagonal of a blackboard is too long to be measured by a standard measuring tape. That said, can you find out the approximate diameter if the said blackboard is 15 feet across and 6 feet in length?

A. 90
B. 16
C. 21
D. 12

19. You are helping a student to find the surface area of the square pyramid given in the visual. To facilitate the calculation, you explain to the student that the four triangular faces are the same. What is the correct formula for calculating the surface area using your hint?

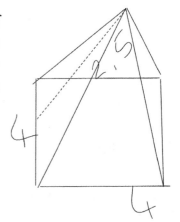

A. Surface area = ½ (4*2.5)*4+ 4*4
B. Surface area = (4*2.5)*4+ 4*4
C. Surface area = 4*(4*2.5)* (4/2)
D. Surface area = ½ (4*2.5)*4

20. If a student wants to isolate the variables in the following equation, what would you advise them?

5= x+7

A. Ask the student to isolate x and show them how they could do it. For instance, they may subtract 7 from both sides of the equation.

B. You will ask them to add 5 to both sides of the equation if they are to isolate 5.

C. Advise how easily the student can isolate x by subtracting 5 from both sides of the equation.

D. Tell the student to isolate x by adding 7 to both sides of the equation.

21. You, as a paraprofessional, are helping a student to plot points (–5, 7) on the coordinate plane. How do you do it?

A. You start at the origin, that is 0 on the coordinate plane, move down 5, and then move up 7.

B. You start at the origin, that is 0 on the coordinate plane, move up 7, then move down 5

C. You start at the origin, that is 0 on the coordinate plane, move to the left side 5, then go right 7

D. You start at the origin, that is 0 on the coordinate plane, move to left 5, then go up 7.

22. One of your students has to find the median of a set of numbers. The student is confused because the set has an even number among the odds. If the set is {5, 7, 8, 9, 11, 13}, how can you help the student to find the median in the set?

A. You will tell the student that there is no median in the set because each number is present only once.

B. There are two medians, 8 and 9.

C. The student should find the average of 8, and 9, the two middle numbers.

D. The student must add all the numbers and then divide the sum obtained by 6.

23. You wrote a question on the blackboard and asked your students to compare the two numbers 0.4, and ¼. You told your students that the method to compare the two would be to write both the numbers as fractions with a common denominator. Which of the following answers did students give correctly to represent the two numbers 0.4, and¼?

A. 4/10, and 1/10
B. 4/10, and 10/40
C. 10/40, and 1/40
D. 10/40, and 1/40

24. Solve the equation, 5x–12= –8, by finding the value of the variable, x.

   A. x= ⅘
   B. x=0.020
   C. x=2
   D. x=4

25. Julian and his friend went to a diner. Julian ordered hash browns for himself and a double cheeseburger for his friend. The cost of hash browns is $2.99, and that of the cheeseburger is $3.89. They also ordered two milkshakes, each costing $2.25. While paying the bill, Julian included a 15% tip. How much did Julian pay the waiter as a tip?

   A. $1.70
   B. $1.65
   C. $7.55
   D. $3

26. The two angles of an isosceles triangle measure 25° and 130°. What should be the measurement of the third angle?

   A. 120°
   B. 45°
   C. 25°
   D. 30°

27. What should be the next term in this geometric sequence of numbers, –2, 6, –18, 54, –162, ?

   A. 81
   B. 486
   C. –486
   D. –1458

28. Two points plotted on the coordinate plane are (–6, 4) and (4, –2). What is the distance between the two points?

   A. 10

B. 18

C. 40

D. 60

29. Answer the following questions from the scores of an English test taken for the sixth grade of your school.

You are given the scores on an English test, 56, 65, 58, 69, 72, 88, 90, 32, 74, 80.

i) Which of these data points is probably an outlier?

A. 90

B. 56

C. 22

D. 80

ii) What is the range of the data provided?

A. 22

B. 90

C. 68

D. 74

30. 50 students took a 6 question quiz. The teacher made a data-table of their scores out of 6 versus the frequency of each score. Which of these will be equal to 50?

A. the sum of both the scores on the table and the frequencies

B. the sum of scores in the data-table

C. the sum of frequencies in the data-table

D. None of these.

31. Where is the number 10/7 located on the number line?

A. between 0 and 1,

B. between 1 and 2,

C. between 2 and 3,

D. between 0 and -1.

32. Clara buys bags of manure for her garden. She had $480 with her, and she wanted to buy as many bags of manure as possible. The cost of the manure is $12 per bag. Clara agreed to pay a delivery charge of $30 for work ease. How many bags of manure did she buy after paying the delivery charges?

    A. 40 bags
    B. 12 bags
    C. 37 bags
    D. 35 bags.

33. Henry buys eight pens at $2.20 per pen. Which of the following options suggest the change he would receive if he bought them using a $30 bill?

    A. $30–(8*$2.20).
    B. ($30–8)* $2.20
    C. $30+(8*$2.20)
    D. ($30–$2.20)*8.

34. Carolyn can read a book in x hours. What portion of the book can she finish in 20 minutes?

    A. 20/x
    B. 20–x
    C. (60–20)/x
    D. (1/60x)*20

Answer Key

Reading

Q	A	Q	A
1	D	18	D
2	A=ii), B=i), C=ii), D=i)	19	C
3	3.	20	B
4	i) T, ii) F, iii) T, iv) F, v) T, vi) F, vii) F	21	D
5	i) O, ii) O, iii) O, iv) O, v) O, vi) F, vii) O, viii) F.	22	D
6	F.	23	A
7	D.	24	D
8	II)	25	D
9	B.	26	C
10	D.	27	C
11	E.	28	A
12	D.	29	D
13	C.	30	B
14	C.	31	D
15	D.	32	B
16	D.	33	C
17	C.	34	B

Writing

Q	A	Q	A
1	B	18	B
2	D	19	D
3	C	20	B
4	D	21	D
5	A	22	B
6	C	23	A
7	A	24	B
8	C	25	I) C, II) B, III) B, IV) C, V) C.
9	C	26	I) B, II) A, III) B
10	B	27	B
11	A	28	A
12	D	29	A
13	C	30	B
14	B	31	C
15	C	32	C
16	D	33	I) B, II) B, III) D
17	C	34	I) B, II) D, III) A.

Math

Q	1	2	3	4	5	6	7	8	9	10	11	12	13	14
A	D	C	C	B	A	B	C	B	D	C	B	D	B	B

Q	15	16	17	18	19	20	21	22	23	24	25	26	27	28
A	C	A	D	B	B	A	D	C	B	A	A	C	B	D

Q	29	30	31	32	33	34
A	I) C. II) C.	C	B	C	A	D

Answer Key and Explanations

Reading

1. **D**

    Definitely is a fact.

2.
    A. the correct answer is ii) opinion
    B. the correct answer is i) fact
    C. the correct answer is ii) opinion
    D. the correct answer is i) fact

3. Answer 3 is correct. Both D and E are facts

4.
    i) is true (opinion)
    ii) is false (not an opinion)
    iii) is true (an opinion)
    iv) is false (not an opinion)
    v) is true (opinion)
    vi) is false (not an opinion)
    vii) is false (not an opinion)

5.
    i) opinion
    ii) opinion
    iii) opinion
    iv) opinion
    v) opinion
    vi) fact
    vii) opinion
    viii) fact

6. **F**

Basil is a herb and not a spice

7. **D**

If the question seems confusing, try to paraphrase it.

8. **ii)**

Proofreading is an organizational skill.

9. **B**

The text helps us to understand the attitude of a filmmaker.

10. **D**

This question checks your ability to recognize the supporting detail in the passage.

11. **E**

This question checks your ability to recognize the organization of the passage. The last sentence describes best the organization of three passages. In the first sentence fragment, we learn that a problematic issue is being discussed in the text, which is true. The second part of the sentence is also true because the text does not offer any concrete way to derive energy from the sea-based windmills.

12. **D**

This question tests if you can find the relationship between the ideas that are mentioned in the two passages about a topic. Both the passages tell us about ecotourism and its environmental impacts when properly managed.

13. **C**

Two ideas are presented in the passages of the text. The question tests your ability to find a relationship between the ideas. While the first passage gives a general account about how we can do ecotourism effectively, the next passage gives a specific example of ecotourism.

14. **C**

This particular question tests whether you can locate the specific details mentioned in a passage and compare the ways the author has taken to discuss a topic. The first passage tells us about the economic influence of ecotourism on the local population. Other than c), no other options clearly describe the difference between the two passages.

15. **D**

The height or length of each component of the bar chart represents the number of units or observations in the said category or states the value of the variable. From the diagram, we can see that vandalism was the least in 2016.

16. **D**

The inference may be that the after-school programs may help in declining crime rates, but at best, it is a probability. The text does not mention that the audience is persuaded about the effects of after-school programs. The text does not mention anything about funding programs in school. However, it explains that in this particular town, petty crime rates declined following the implementation of the after-school programs.

17. **C**

The height or length of each component of the bar chart represents the number of units or observations in the said category or states the value of the variable.

18. **D**

The crime rates decreased in 2016, as is shown by the bar diagrams.

19. **C**

There were no extra expenditures mentioned in the paragraph, the police did not announce any punitive steps for not participating in a voluntary event, and the students did not express any desire to spend extra hours after school.

20. **B**

Paying students for going to school is a "great idea" suggests that the statement is an opinion and not a fact.

21. **D**

Those people who are concerned and relevant to the idea.

22. **D**

The main idea of this passage is that paying students to attend school might help decrease the dropout rate of kids who feel they need a paycheck to help pay family bills.

23. **A**

The text mentions why the idea of paying students to attend school is a good one, but the absence of a counterargument from the opponents of this view means the text lacks persuasion. A persuasive text may not include a conclusive paragraph, although some hint at a conclusion should be present. The text includes a thesis component: *One method to address this problem is to pay the students for school attendance.* The text provides supporting evidence for the idea it mentioned in the text.

24. **D**

A graph to illustrate recent dropout rates would provide a visual to the reader of the extent of the problem. A bar graph of American poverty levels isn't an appropriate choice because everyone living in poverty doesn't have a high school-aged child in their household.

A pie chart of the future plans of high school graduates is not helpful because the text is concerned with students who drop out and never graduate. A pie chart to indicate the most popular majors among high school students is not related to the topic.

25. **D**

This is the only option that tells the communication system of dolphins gives an insight into their intelligence.

26. **C**

The text tells us about the dolphin communication system, choice C is correct.

27. **C**

Refer to the use of the word "vocalization" in the text. It tells about both clicks and whistles. It is about making meaningful sounds.

28. **A**

The text is in chronological order—the order of time. It takes us through the events as they happened over time.

29. **D**

The author is explaining the nature of humorous stories.

30. **B**

    While other stories can be engaging, humorous stories, according to the text, are most difficult to write.

31. **D**

    Humorous stories, according to the text, are most challenging to write; the text does not tell us about other stories being non-engaging.

32. **B**

    While A and D are not correct in the paragraph's context, C is more tempting. However, the author clearly stated the supremacy of humorous story-telling over a comic one.

33. **C**

    The humor in the humorous stories may be wry and often implied. It is not overly expressed as in comic stories.

34. **B**

    The author is trying to tell us about how visual perception occurs. Vision is an active process; the author wants us to be aware of and not afraid of the blind spot. X and O are used to identify the blind spot.

Writing

1. **B**

    Writing in a passive voice is a matter of personal choice. That said, an Active voice is more engaging with the readers. When you write in an active voice, you use the subject to do the action. The readers feel the action happening. For instance, "I saw Sarah in the market." Writing this sentence in a passive voice, "Sarah was seen by me in the market," seems both distant and formal.

2. **D**

The complete predicate in a sentence has a verb and all the words that modify or explain the verb. The first sentence has no verb, and the second sentence also lacks a verb. The second part of the third sentence is an independent clause having its own subject and a verb.

3. **C**

The appropriate choice should be a semicolon, in the absence of which we may rewrite the sentence by splitting them up. A semicolon does not need the use of coordinating conjunctions between two independent clauses. If we use a comma, we must put coordinating conjunctions like "and." Colons are used when the second clause explains or cites the first clause as an example.

4. **D**

Up is a preposition. Prepositions explain the temporal or positional relationship between two things in a sentence. In this sentence, up shows the relationship between the cat and the tree.

5. **A**

Don't feel embarrassed because you tripped and fell in front of the entire class. The word tripped is misspelled.

6. **C**

Family titles like uncle, aunt, and grandma needs capitalization when used as a part of someone's specific name, like Uncle John. When you use them to clarify relationships, you don't need to capitalize them. An example of the latter would be, "Jim went to the market with his uncle."

Seasons are not proper names and need not be capitalized. When you begin a new sentence, you start with a capital letter even when it is in the context of a longer sentence, as is the example with the quote from Mom. Acronyms (NASA) are always capitalized along with the names of months.

7. **A**

It should be its.

8. **C**

Mary does not agree with the pronoun "his."

9. **C**

Words in a title are generally capitalized unless they are an article. This exception occurs when the articles come at the beginning of a title. Coordinating conjunction, unless used as the first word of a title, or prepositions shorter than four letters need not be capitalized. "Through" is capitalized because it is longer than four letters.

10. **B**

A should be "accept" and not except, C should use "lose," and not loose, and D should use "than" instead of then.

11. **A**

Prewriting is the stage when the writer plans and decides what they are going to write about a subject. In the revising stage, students need to evaluate the content of the text— sufficient examples are present, the transitions are functional, and the text is coherent. Finally, the message must be clear. In editing, the student is required to find out mechanical errors. Once everything is inspected and checked, the text is published. The readers then enjoy it.

12. **D**

The four core purposes of writing are to inform, entertain, persuade, and express feelings. It is up to the readers to get impressed by the writing.

13. **C**

Persuasive writing tries to persuade or convince the reader to agree with the author. Argumentative writing wants the reader to acknowledge the validity of the author's argument but not necessarily be convinced by it or persuaded to believe it.

Narrative writing is the true art of storytelling which tells a story. It is usually for the purpose of entertainment.

Descriptive writing describes something using details and imagination that helps the reader form a mental picture of the text.

14. **B**

Knowing the reader answers the questions about why and for whom you are penning the book.

15. **C**

Option C is an individual opinion. You may not agree with the author, but their source can still be credible.

16. **D**

16. Atlases are maps that carry a lot of information, including the migration pattern of people. Dictionaries are good for searching the meaning of words, and a Thesaurus for synonyms. Primary source documents do not exist for ancient civilizations, and may have been destroyed, lost, or not deciphered.

17. **C**

Students will need guidance to locate their mistakes. The teacher should guide the student to the part they have made mistakes and encourage them to identify them by asking guiding questions.

18. **B**

"James mentioned Tracy could come with him for a ride in the text." This sentence lacks clarity. The sentence needs rewriting as "James mentioned in the text that Tracy could come with him for a ride."

19. **D**

A thesaurus is a book that gives you synonyms for different words.

20. **B**

There should be a question mark after 'you.'

21. **D**

it should be "her *to* move" rather than her move and "fewer" rather than had less.

22. **B**

Unthinkingly qualifies the verb grabbed and is an adverb.

23. **A**

Salivary

24. **B**

Predicate has a verb and states something about the subject.

25. **i) C**

Nevertheless is the correct choice. Therefore is a wrong choice because the first part of the sentence does not explain the second clause. Two contrasting professions, the blue-collar working class and the white-collar professionals are best offset by *nevertheless* in this context. It is a contrasting conjunction.

ii) B

Please note that the World cup must be capitalized, and hence, D is wrong.

iii) B

since it avoids redundancy.

iv) C

The statement is a general one, and using "they" is more inclusive.

v) C

Hotter in comparison to what? When you are writing, you must be careful about the choice of words.

26. **i) B**

A non-quoted clause or phrase should be set off by a comma on both sides when placed in the middle of a quote mark. There should be no comma between a noun and its modifying prepositional phrase or between an adjective and the noun phrase it modifies.

ii) A

Use a comma after an interjection.

iii) B

A modifying phrase between a subject and predicate should be set off by commas on both sides.

27. **B**

There should be quotation marks on both sides, and they should be inside the parenthesis.

28. **A**

Use of the present perfect tense is ok because the action is not yet finished.

29. **A**

The adverb form is "Perfectly.". We use this when modifying a verb, in this case, did. The verb can come before ("did perfectly") or after ("perfectly accomplished"). The position of the verb depends on personal preference or contextual tone.

30. **A**

Both A and b) look good, but A uses "has reached," which is a wrong use of the verb in this context.

31. **C**

Affected is the verb. Changes is a plural noun.

32. **C**

This is conditional-subjunctive construction where "if" introduces the conditional clause or phrase— the main clause of the sentence. It is conditional on the dependent clause and the corresponding subjunctive should not use the form would have.

33. **i) B**

Committee is a collective noun and should be singular.

ii) B

Since the sentence mentions "boys." we may use the pronoun his.

iii) D

each of **us** has our **own**.

34. **i) B**

Euphemism is a style of language that departs from being straightforward, its use may make a text illogical.

ii) D

Evoke means induce

iii) A

A lyre is a medieval string instrument.

Math

1. **D**

The square root of a square is just the length of one of its sides because all its sides are equal. If n is a side, the square is represented by n raised to the power 2, or n2. The square root will be expressed as √n.

In our example, the number of unit squares making a side is the square root of the square. Let us say, for example, the square has 5 unit squares on each side. The big square representing 5 squared will be 25. The square root of 25 is 5, the number of unit squares on each side.

2. **C**

70% means 70 out of 100 of the tank is full. Thus, 100-70=30 parts out of 100 is empty. It can be represented as 30/100 or 3/10.

3. **C**

The smallest integers are those that have the greatest **absolute values**. Let us write the negative integers first, from least to the greatest.

{-8, -7 ⅘, -3}.

9/50 = 0.18 which should come next. Therefore, we may write as {-8, -7 ⅘, -3, 9/50}

The next larger number is 0.25. 5/2 or 2.5 is the largest of all.

Thus we may write the set as{ -8, -7 ⅘, -3, 9/50, 0.25, 5/2}in order from the least to the largest number.

4. **B**

In a number line, the thousandth place is the third digit to the right from the decimal. The hundredth place precedes it, and the tenth place comes before that. On the left-hand side of the number line, we have the tens, hundreds, and thousands place, which must not be confused with the -dths.

In this diagram, d in the center is the decimal. Those on its left are the positions for tens, hundreds, and thousands; on the right are corresponding tenths, hundredth, and the thousandth place.

5. **A**

40% is 0.40 when expressed in decimal. The equation can be written as 0.40✕80=32

6. **B**

Since the question asks for an approximate value, we can safely round off the numbers like 550 and 21.

550.4=550; we round down the figure because 4 in the tenth's place is less than 5. The whole number after removing the fraction is, therefore, 550.

20.496 can be rounded up as 20.45. This again can be rounded up as 20.5 because of the number in the hundredth place, 5. Finally, 20.5 can be rounded up as the whole number 21 because the digit after the decimal is 5.

If you multiply 550 with 21, the closest answer is 11,000.

7. **C**

The dotted line is not to divide the triangle. It is the height of the triangle essential to determine its area.

The formula for area A= ½ Base✕Height

Or, ½ ✕10✕8

Or, 40 square inches.

8. **B**

The sum appears daunting, but proceeding with it according to the rule of PEMDAS can help to solve it easily.

According to the rule, we need to solve the bracket and the exponent first. The equation can be written as, [(84×84)÷28×12]÷24=7x

Or, 7x=[84×3×12]÷24

Or, 7x=42×3

Or, x=42×3/7

Or, x=18

9. **D**

We will again follow the PEMDAS rule to solve this equation and find the value of x.

x= -224+ (-314)×(-9)

We must do the multiplication first to solve the equation. The rule is when we are multiplying a negative number with a positive number, the value is always negative. However, we get a positive product number when multiplying two negative or two positive numbers.

Or x=-224+2826.

Or, x=2602

10. **C**

Following the rule of PEMDAS, we may write the equation as $(4)^2+15 \div 5$

In the next step, we must solve the exponent. $4^2=16$

The next step would be to divide.

16+3

or, 19.

Reviewing the PEMDAS rule, we may consider doing the operation in a step-by-step manner given below.

P= Do everything in parentheses (P), left to right.

E= Evaluate any exponents (E), left to right.

M and D= Do all multiplication and division MD), in order, left to right.

A and S= Do all addition and subtraction (AS), in order, from left to right.

A good way to remember the rule is **P**lease **E**xcuse **M**y **D**ear **A**unt **S**ally

11. **B**

   To find the value for x, you have to shift 4 to the other side of the equal sign. When you do that, you write the equation as –x= 16/4

   Or, –x= 4

   Or, x=–4

12. **D**

   There is a negative number in the given set{–4, 0, 4, 8, 12, 16}.

   The total sum value of the set is 36. We can break up the operation as follows.

   The first and the third number of the set give 0.

   –4 and 4=0.

   If we add 0 with the second number of the set, which is 0 we get 0.

   0+0=0

   Effectively, the set is the sum of the last three numbers, 8, 12, and 16.

   (8+12+16)=36

   However, there are six numbers in the set. We are required to find the **mean** value of the set. It is an **average** of **all** the numbers given in the set, including zero. There are six numbers in the set. Hence, we divide 36 (sum) with 6 (the number of digits in the set).

   The value of the set is 6.

13. **B**

As you follow the numbers carefully, you can find that the value decreases from left to right. Find the difference between any two consecutive numbers going from left to right. The difference is 5. Therefore, we may write the sequence as 9, 4, –1, —, –11

Or the missing number between –1 and –11 can only be five less than –1.

If you consult a number line, the next digit in this equation after –1 is –6.

14. **B**

You have to put the value for the x-coordinate and then that for the y-coordinate. The point, P, is on 1 in the x-coordinate and -2 on the y-coordinate.

15. **C**

Follow the "trend" of Martha's reading habits closely. We will find that she finishes one book per month. Do not use only the first data point when making predictions. Look at the overall trend, which in this case has increased by one book per month. So, it is safe to assume that she will finish 7 books in 7 months.

16. **A**

The volume of a rectangular prism $V = H \times L \times W$

Or, $V = 2 \times 8 \times 2$

Or, $V = 32$

Volume is always expressed in cubic units. It can be understood if we multiply only the units. inches×inches×inches.

17. **D**

   The sum tells about two different kinds of operation, subtraction, and addition. A parenthesis must separate them. The second set of parenthesis is required to maintain the consistency of the statement.

   You have to remember that you are not asked to solve the problem but to express the mathematical statement in proper number sequence; in other words, you are writing the equation.

18. **B**

   You can use the Pythagorean theorem to find out the diameter of this blackboard, which for a rectangle, is as follows.

   $d^2 = l^2 + w^2$,

   where d= the diameter of a rectangle, l is the length, and w is its width. Now, substituting the variables' values, we may write the equation as follows.

   $d^2 = 15^2 + 6^2$

   $d^2 = 225 + 36$

   Or, $d^2 = 261$

   Or, d= 16 (approx.)

   The diameter of the blackboard is 16 feet.

19. **B**

   The area of each triangle is given by the formula as follows.

   Area (A)= ½ *b*h, where b=base of the square and h= height.

   Therefore, the area of one triangle is ½*4*2.5.

The formula for the area of any triangle is not just the right triangle. If you do not divide by ½ you will get the value of the entire rectangle with dimensions 4 and 2.5.

We have to multiply ½*4*2.5 by 4 and then add the area of the square at the base. The area of the square is 4*4

Therefore, the correct formula is Surface area = (4*2.5)*4+ 4*4

If in the examination you have been asked to find the surface area of a solid figure, take it for granted that the base is included unless the question mentions otherwise.

20. **A**

The variable in this equation is x, and the rest are constants. Therefore, the student has to isolate x from the equation. Of all the options suggested above, choice A is most appropriate. When you subtract the same number digit from both sides of the equation, the equation remains undisturbed. Let us write it out.

5= x+7

By subtracting 7 from both sides, we have 5–7= x+7–7. Essentially the equation remains the same as 5=x+7 because 5–7= x+7–7 is the same as 5–7+7 =x+7. The action opposite to addition is subtraction.

However, your purpose is to help the student identify the variable and the correct method to find its value. Option A is the correct choice. b) is wrong because 5 is not a variable; it's a constant. Let us find out what happens to the equation when we subtract 5 from both sides of the equation.

5–5=x+7–5

In this case, the equation when solved becomes zero on the left side.

0=x+7–5. You cannot *isolate* x. Note that the question has asked you to *isolate* the *variables*. The purpose of the question is **not** to find out the value of x.

21. **D**

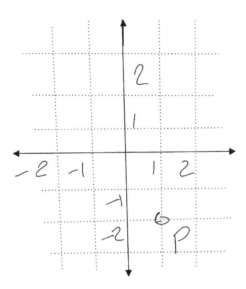

Let us consider the graph in the visual aid. While on the x-coordinate, the negative signs move to the left from zero, on the y-coordinate, the positive signs move up from zero.

x is always left and right, and y is always up and down. When we plot, we mention the x-coordinate first, and the y comes next.

(x-coordinate, y-coordinate) = (–5, 7)

A. is the wrong option because both the values would be plotted on the y-axis.

B. is wrong because both the values would be plotted in the y-axis; besides, it would change the signs of the numerals.

C. is a wrong choice because both the values would be plotted on the x-axis

22. **C**

Median means middle. In this set, there is no single middle number. However, 8, and 9 are closest to the middle. Therefore, the middle number of the set {5, 7, 8, 9, 11, 13} should be an average of 8, and 9.

Option d) is wrong because the operation would give us the mean value of the set and not the median.

23. **B**

The first step is to change both the numbers into fractions. While ¼ is already present as a fraction, we need to convert only 0.4 to its fraction state. 0.4=4/10

Therefore, we may write the numbers as 4/10, and ¼.

The easiest way to compare two fractions would be to make their denominators the same. The least common denominator 4/10, and ¼ is 40.

We can multiply the denominator of the second number ¼ by 10. But we need to multiply the numerator by the same number in order to keep the fraction intact.

1*10/4*10

Or, 10/40, or ¼ .

Now let us consider the first number 0.4, which we wrote as a fraction: 4/10. We may write the two numbers side by side and compare.

4/10, 10/40

Obviously, we need to multiply the denominator of the first fraction by 4. It means we must multiply the numerator (4) by the same number to keep the fraction's value intact.

4*4/10*4

Or, 16/40, or 4/10, or 0.4

Finally, you may place the numbers side by side and compare.

16/40 and 10/40

You can see that 16/40 is more than 10/40.

Do a little back-calculation by converting both values to their decimals, 16/40 =0.4, and 10/40=0.25. Obviously, 0.4 is more than 0.25

24. **A**

We can solve the equation in the following method.

5x–12= –8,

Or, 5x= –8+12,

Or, 5x= 4

Or, x=⅘

Option b) is wrong because when converted to decimal, ⅘= 0.2

25. **A**

Add the total bill amount. Julian paid $11.38 for their meal. He included a 15% tip on $11.38. You are asked how much Julian paid the waiter as a tip. To find out 15% of 11.38, you must multiply 11.38 by 0.15. 11.38 can be written as 11.4; hence, A is a better choice than b). Choice b) considers 11.38 as 11.3, which is wrong.

Note, do not multiply 11.38 by 15 and divide by 100 to find the value. In that case, as shown in option C, you will end up paying the waiter more than you intended.

26. **C**

The two angles and corresponding two sides of an isosceles triangle are equal. They are called congruent angles. The total sum value of all the angles in a triangle is 180°. Therefore, A is wrong. Only C is correct because it corresponds to one of the angles. Therefore, the angle measurements for this isosceles triangle are 25°, 25°, and 130°.

27. **B**

A geometric sequence, also known as a geometric progression, is a sequence of numbers or terms that are not zero. After the first one, each term is obtained by multiplying the preceding term by a fixed number. Consider the set given in the question –2, 6, –18, 54, –162, ?

The second term 6 can be found by multiplying –2 by –3. Only when two negatives are multiplied do we get a positive number. The second term is 6. Multiply it by –3 again. You get the third term –18. Multiply it by –3 to get 54.

54, when multiplied by –3, gives –162. We must now multiply –162 by –3 to arrive at the term in question. Multiplying the two gives you 486. It is a positive number because you are multiplying two negatives.

28. **D**

The following formula for distance calculates the distance between two points.

$$\sqrt{(x_2 - x_1)^2 (y_2 - y_1)^2}$$

In the sum that has been given to us, x1= –6, y1= 4, x2= 4, and y2= –2

By substituting the variable with the values given in the question, we get

Or, d=√ [4–(–6)]2*[(–2)–4]2

Or, d= √(10)2*(–6)2

Or, d=√100*36

Or d=√3600

Or, d=√10*10*6*6

Or, d=60

29. **i) C**

An outlier is a data point having a value that differs from other data values to a significant extent. We are able to pick out the outlier when we arrange the data values in increasing order.

22, 56, 58, 65, 69, 72, 74, 80, 88, 90. While the majority of the values fall between 56 and 90, 22 is definitely out of the group being 36 less than the value of the next number.

ii) C

The range of a set of data is the difference between the maximum value and the minimum value given in the data set. In this data set, the maximum value is 90, and the minimum is 22. Their difference is 68.

30. **C**

Frequency refers to the number of students who received each score. Since we add up all of the numbers of students who got the scores, we get 50, the number of students.

31. **B**

$10/7 = 1^3/_7$, which is greater than 1, but less than 2. Therefore, b) is the correct choice.

32. **C**

Clara could have bought 40 bags if she did not order home delivery. She had to subtract the delivery charge of $30 from the amount of $480 she had with her. After paying the delivery charge, Clara was left with $450. The cost of each bag of manure was $12; she could buy only 37 bags.

33. **A**

You will find out the cost of eight pens. The cost is $2.20*8.

You give the storekeeper your $30 bill. He keeps the cost of eight pens and returns the change to you. Hence, the first equation is the correct expression of the operation.

34. **D**

Carolyn reads in x hours, or 60x minutes 1 book.

Or, in 1 minute, she reads 1/60x

In 20 minutes, Carolyn reads (1/60x)*20 pages of the book.

Practice Test #2

Reading

1. Choose if the given words are A "opinion" or b) "fact"?

   A. i) believe
   B. ii) worst
   C. iii) least
   D. iv) wrongly

2. Choose the correct word for the gap in the sentence below.

   Rose is a voracious reader, very —in her taste.

   A. incongruous
   B. eclectic
   C. superfluous
   D. specific

3. *The house is substantial, and its facade is Grecian.*

   In the sentence above, "substantial" means one of the following choices. Identify which one.

   A. neat

B. important

C. concrete

D. grand

4. The aural feature of balance is crucial for control of posture for ambulation. In this context, "Aural" means:

A. Audible

B. Hearsay

C. Halo

D. Ears

5. The wound had a copious purulent discharge. In this context, "Copious" means:

A. Bountiful

B. Expansive

C. Profuse

D. Torrential

6. The student was heedless of the teacher's advice. In this context, "Heedless" means:

A. Deaf

B. Inattentive

C. Selfish

D. Adventurous

Read the following paragraph carefully and then answer questions #7- #14.

Sequoia and Kings Canyon National Parks *support an* extensive range of animal and plant species due to its range of climatic, altitude, and habitat conditions. The number of native *vertebra species* in the park exceeds 250. There may be many more that have not been discovered yet. Five of the native vertebra species are extinct, and more than 150 are *endangered*. It is not known how many species of invertebrates are present in the park. In some of its caves, some species of invertebrates are found that are unobtainable worldwide. In the foothills of the National Park, where there is hot and dry summer and mild winter, plant life is *largely chaparral*. Blue oak and California buckeye can be found in the valleys and higher slopes. Many animals are permanent residents of these areas; <u>some breed, others winter</u>. Local species include gray fox, bobcat, striped and spotted skunks, black bear, wood rat, pocket gopher, white-footed mouse, and birds like California quail, scrub jay, lesser goldfinch, wrentit, acorn woodpecker, gopher snake, California king snake, striped racer, wester whiptail lizard, and the California newt.

7. What is the author's purpose in writing this passage

    A. to tire the reader.
    B. to convince the reader.
    C. to give information.
    D. to entertain the reader.

8. The word support from the text mostly means

    A. accredit
    B. produce
    C. protect
    D. foster

9. What does the author mean by vertebra species?

    A. snakes
    B. birds
    C. bears
    D. all of the above

10. "There may be many more that have not been discovered yet."

    Who is the author referring to?

    A. fishes
    B. flowers
    C. invertebrates
    D. vertebrates

11. "Endangered" in this context means

    A. dangerous, involving risks

     B. spoiled

     C. in danger of extinction

     D. unsteady

12. The marked part of the sentence <u>unobtainable worldwide.</u> in context to the passage, best means

     A. are indigenous only to these National Parks

     B. Are not found anywhere in the world.

     C. The author is referring to the animal species of the National Parks.

     D. The author is telling us about the rarity of invertebrate species worldwide.

13. To find the meaning of the word *chaparral,* what book should be the best choice to consult?

     A. A Thesaurus

     B. A Dictionary

     C. The Glossary of the book

     D. An Encyclopedia

14. What do you think the author implies when he mentions, "<u>some breed, others winter.</u>"

     A. the author is talking about some animal breeds and the winter months in the parks.

     B. the author is talking about the genealogy of the animals.

     C. some animals find the park a good breeding ground, and others spend the harsh winter.

     D. some animals reproduce, and others take a short break.

Read the following text carefully and then answer questions #15- #17.

Nancy Maynor once argued that e-mails had created their own style of language. She coined the term "e-style" for this mode of writing letters. Maynor's research suggested that e-style was more similar to spoken words than written. E-mails are usually informally written using clipped words like "lingo" for language. This informality is also seen in the case of punctuation. The ten common punctuation peculiarities that Maynor noticed in the e-mails include lack of capitalization, excessive use of exclamation marks, and recurring use of dots and dashes that trail at the end of the sentences. Maynor came to the conclusion that these traits give a distinct conversational tint to e-mail messages.

15. The text's main purpose is one of the following. Which one do you think fits better the text's purpose?

    A. To tell us about the research work of Maynor.
    B. To present the contrast between two theories.
    C. criticize the e-mails.
    D. question the conclusion.

16. Maynor concluded that the characteristics of punctuation marks in the e-mail messages denote one of the following flavors of writing messages. Which of the following choices do you think is the most concerning feature of punctuation marks in e-mails?

    A. the messages become unreadable.
    B. the correspondence is unacceptable for informal communication.
    C. the style is more conversational.
    D. the style reflects archaic English

17. You will find "lingo" in the passage. What do you think the word stands for concerning the passage?

    A. Spellings characteristic to e-mail messages only.
    B. the casual style of e-mails.
    C. words that render reading e-mail problematic.
    D. one of the punctuation features peculiar to e-mails.

18. Owing to diversity, there is hardly any scope to expound a systematic account of liberalism in its many forms and variants. Which word best describes Expound:

    A. Sidestep
    B. Calculate
    C. Describe
    D. Write down

19. Instead of acting on impulse, it is best to dissect a problem. The word dissect in this context means:

    A. Avoid
    B. Face
    C. Analyze
    D. Supervise

20. Most of the high school students maintained a serious countenance while the kids laughed. In this context, Countenance means:

    A. Discipline
    B. Power
    C. Seniority
    D. Expression

21. Choose which of the following terms is "opinion?"

    A. correctly
    B. possibly
    C. recognized
    D. occurred

22. Choose which of the following is "fact?"

    A. most
    B. usually
    C. in my perspective
    D. did

23. Choose which of the following is "fact?"

    A. always
    B. will
    C. intelligent
    D. expect

Read the following paragraph and then answer the questions #24 and #25

When Lyndon Johnson was young, his father once told him that he should be able to tell those people who supported him and who were against as soon as he entered into a room. Otherwise, politics was not his cup of tea. Intelligent as he was, <u>even Johnson did not possess such supernatural power</u>. However, he liked to narrate this story. This tells us something about his personality; he depended on instinct. In his Presidential career, he often turned to his instincts. It was developed in the Texas hill country, cultivated in his political life, and validated in an extended and respected congressional career. He would learn to trust his instincts while in the White House. His reliance on intuition enabled Johnson to wear the presidency like a familiar suit.

24. Which of the following word, if exchanged for "supernatural," would not alter the meaning of the marked part of the text?

    A. historical
    B. uncanny
    C. unrevealed
    D. strange

25. The author is primarily focused on

    A. explaining a mental faculty.
    B. making comparisons
    C. stating facts
    D. repeating a story

26. You, as a paraprofessional, have asked your students to sound words in a column. Which of the following words does not make a long "oo" vowel sound?

    A. misunderstood
    B. sharpshooter
    C. tablespoon
    D. bloodcurdling

27. You, as a paraprofessional, are teaching your students about "root words." Which of the following is the root word for dismal?

    A. dis-
    B. -mal
    C. d-
    D. di-

28. Identify the root word for "confinement"

    A. con-
    B. fine
    C. -ment
    D. fin

29. What is the root word for rephrased?

    A. Re-
    B. phrase
    C. phrased
    D. -ed

30. Which pair of words are correctly synonymous?

    A. feel and felt
    B. hurt and sore
    C. come and go
    D. prise and prize
    E. new and knew

Read the passage and then answer questions #31, and #32.

The Trojan War hero was Achilles, who was believed to be a demi-god. Everyone respected him, including Hector and Paris, who were his rivals. Achilles' general was Agamemnon. He thought differently about Achilles. Agamemnon believed that it was he who deserved everyone's attention because he was the general. Hence he summoned a muster; all the soldiers gathered together to hear Agamemnon.

31. In the text, the word "muster" can be best explained by which word from the text?

    A. general
    B. summoned
    C. gathered
    D. deserved.

32. If you are told to arrange all the proper names from the passage in alphabetical order, how would you arrange them?

    A. *Achilles, Agamemnon, Hector, and Paris.*
    B. *Agamemnon, Achilles, Hector, and Paris.*
    C. *Achilles, Hector, Paris, and Agamemnon.*
    D. *Hector, Paris, Achilles, and Agamemnon.*

33. Some degree of caution while analyzing the data is justified; however, one should not ignore the government's record.

    In the sentence given above, you have to look up the dictionary to understand the meaning of the word justified. On which of the following pages can you find the word?

    A. page 712 ("job-jobholder")
    B. page 714 ("justice-justness")
    C. page 713 ("just-justice")
    D. page 715("justification-justify")

34. The United States began restricting trade with the Japanese ahead of the Pearl Harbor attack. They made it difficult for the Japanese to trade with other countries. The Japanese had no choice but to attack Pearl Harbor, a United States naval base in Hawaii, on December 7, 1941. This convinced the United States to join World War II formally.

    You, as a paraprofessional, guide your students to "arrange the events of the passage in chronological order." A student writes, "The United States enters World War II." How did they misunderstand the direction?

    A. They thought the direction was to list things in order of importance.

B. They picked the event that is first listed and not the one that happened at first.

C. They listed an event that is out of context.

D. They thought they should list the events in alphabetical order

Writing

1. Identify the part of speech in the underlined section of the following sentence:

   Meena said she was too busy with her work to attend my birthday party, <u>yet</u> she was seen shopping in the supermarket by Jerry this evening.

   A. adjective
   B. conjunction
   C. interjection
   D. preposition

2. What is the most important thing to do in the prewriting stage?

   A. Write well-formed paragraphs citing enough pieces of evidence in favor.
   B. Write down all the ideas, although you may not use all of them in your writing.
   C. Check spelling and grammar.
   D. Ensure you are writing complete sentences.

3. Which bolded portions in the following sentence have grammatical construction, word use, punctuation, or capitalization errors?

   Clara Barton, who founded the **American Red Cross** in 1881, created an organization that **has been serving** the underprivileged for **moreover** 125 years.

   A. has been serving
   B. Clara Barton
   C. moreover
   D. American Red Cross

4. Which bolded portions in the following sentence have grammatical construction, word use, punctuation, or capitalization errors?

   The **Brooklyn Bridge, opened in** May 24, 1883, was the **first fixed crossing** of the **East river**.

   A. Brooklyn Bridge, opened in
   B. first fixed crossing
   C. East river
   D. opened in, East River

5. You, as a paraprofessional, are guiding a student who wrote an essay draft in a passive voice. Which of the following suggestions for the sentence below is the transition to the best active voice?

   English is spoken all over the world.

   A. The world speaks English.
   B. All the world speaks English.
   C. People speak English all over the world.
   D. The whole of the world speaks English.

6. A student finished drafting their essay. Identify the next step in the writing process.

   A. Editing
   B. Publishing
   C. Revising
   D. Prewriting

7. You are guiding a student in reviewing their work on punctuation. You notice a punctuation error in the text. Which sentence does *not* use a semicolon correctly?

   A. Sarah and Deborah went to buy some gifts; but they were getting late for dinner home.
   B. I forgot to bring my umbrella; however, Rita lent me one.
   C. We are having some problems with connection; please stay online.
   D. The cat slept through the storm; the bats flew; the dogs crouched in the shelter.

8. The painting title reads: "watching the ship sail into the Atlantic ocean." Which one of the following titles is correct?

   A. Watching the Ship Sail Into the Atlantic Ocean
   B. Watching the Ship Sail into the Atlantic Ocean
   C. Watching the Ship sail into the Atlantic Ocean
   D. Watching the ship sail into the Atlantic ocean

9. In the sentence below, identify which of the bolded portions has a grammatical error.

   "Shon, the **youngest** of the twins, **was born** almost two minutes after his sister, who was **more eager** to come out **into** the world.

   A. was born
   B. more eager
   C. into
   D. youngest

10. In the following sentence, identify the part of speech of the underlined word:

    The two brothers go <u>everywhere</u> together.

    A. adjective
    B. verb
    C. noun
    D. adverb

11. Which of the following sentences has a spelling error?

    A. It is important to give value to knowledge and expertise and guard against distractions to be successful in life.
    B. Linda finds the cemeteries peaceful places, although the idea may seem weird to many.
    C. The persistent ringing in my ears interfere with my sleep.
    D. I checked the calender to confirm my journey dates.

12. A paraprofessional was revising an essay written by a student. She found an incomplete sentence. What should be her best approach to guide the student to identify their error and correct it?

    A. Show the student which one is the incomplete sentence and ask what is missing that makes the sentence incomplete.
    B. Read the incomplete sentence to the student, then compare the sentence with an adjacent complete sentence, and ask the student to find out the difference between the two sentences.
    C. Review with the student about what makes a sentence complete—then ask the student to go through their text again to identify if there are any incomplete sentences.
    D. Encourage the student to read aloud the text portion with the mistake and see whether the student identifies which sentences are incomplete.

13. Which one of the underlined sections in the text has an error?

    What the dog don't realize, though, was that the cookie was bait to lure him to drop daddy's cap.

    A. was that
    B. the cookie
    C. him to
    D. don't realize

14. Which one of the underlined sections in the text has an error?

    The Baltimore Orioles, an American professional baseball team, won the world series in 1983 after thirteen years without a title.

    A. Baltimore Orioles
    B. won the
    C. world series
    D. in 1983
    E. after thirteen years without

15. What should be the correct preposition in the following sentence?

    The President's speech is broadcast at Independence Day.

    A. At
    B. On
    C. In
    D. Over

16. Identify the word with correct spelling:

    A. Multidisciplinary
    B. Etiqette
    C. Fullfillment
    D. Accomodation

17. Identify the **subject** in the following sentence:

    "The more Sam thought about the incident, the more troubled he became."

    A. He
    B. incident
    C. Sam
    D. thought

18. Which one of the underlined sections from the line has an error?

    Some mention <u>the expression</u> "walking encyclopedia," <u>were inspired</u> only by Hildegard Von Bingen, a woman famous for having <u>a diverse set of</u> expertise and knowledge.

    A. the expression
    B. were inspired
    C. a diverse set of
    D. ,

19. Identify the wrong word or phrases:

Its his prerogative to tell his mother of his whereabouts.

   A. of his
   B. prerogative to
   C. its
   D. whereabouts

20. Identify the conjunction in the following sentence:

I asked her to leave, for I was tired.

   A. Asked
   B. Tired
   C. For
   D. to

21. Find the appropriate word to fill in the blank: The company was — with calls the moment it floated the tender.

   A. Inundated
   B. Superseded
   C. Chastened
   D. Dispossessed

22. Choose the correct pair of words for the following sentence:

His — was noticed by so many of us, and he was so embarrassed by it that he became — in the meeting.

   A. Veracity, unctuous
   B. Effrontery, presumptuous
   C. Altruism, praiseworthy
   D. Gaffe, reticent

23. Identify which of the following sentences is grammatically correct.

    A. You do not keep spaces between each stitch, giving it a continuous appearance hence, it is excellent for securing seams.
    B. You do not keep spaces between each stitch giving it a continuous appearance hence it is excellent for securing seams.
    C. You do not keep spaces between each stitch, giving it a continuous appearance; hence, it is excellent for securing seams.
    D. You do not keep spaces between each stitch, giving it a continuous appearance hence it is excellent for securing seams

24. Identify the sentence with no spelling mistakes.

    A. A back stitch can adapt to curves well and is a low-maintanance stitch.
    B. A back stitch can adopt to curves well and is a low-maintenance stitch.
    C. A back stitch can adept to curves well and is a low maintenance stitch.
    D. A back stitch can adapt to curves well and is a low-maintenance stitch.

25. Choose the sentence with the correct comma usage. The last choice mentions that the sentence is written correctly.

    i) For the Christmas celebration, we were sitting in the dining room, on the front porch and in the backyard.

    A. Christmas, celebration,
    B. were, sitting
    C. porch, and
    D. There is no error.

    ii) Seema seems to be a nice, kind-hearted girl.

    A. seems, to
    B. nice kind-hearted,
    C. nice kind-hearted
    D. No error.

    iii) This book Neil, has seen better days.

A. book, Neil,
B. has, seen
C. Neil
D. No error

iv) My sister has shifted to 118 Mayfield Avenue, Baltimore Maryland 09928.

A. My sister,
B. has shifted,
C. Baltimore,
D. No error

26. Identify the correct sentence:

Everyone in the hospital -including the superintendent and the nurses, ran to the door when the fire victims arrived.

A. nurses, ran
B. nurses:ran
C. nurses has run
D. nurses- ran

27. Identify the correct version of the following sentence: To no ones surprise, Jack turned up late for work today as well.

A. no ones surprise
B. noones surprise
C. no-ones surprise
D. no one's surprise

28. Identify the correct version of the following sentence: After the storm, uprooted lampposts were laying on the pavements.

A. were laying
B. lying
C. were lying
D. were laid

29. Identify the correct version of the following sentence: If you would have read "White Fang," you might have liked Jack London.

    A. would have read
    B. should have read
    C. could have read
    D. had read

30. Identify the correct version of the following sentence: The term boycott derives from Charles C. Boycott, an English realtor based in Ireland that was spurned for refusing to lower the rent.

    A. who was spurned for refusing.
    B. that was spurned for refusing
    C. which was spurned for refusing
    D. who had been spurned for refusing

31. Identify the correct version of the following sentence: Last evening the weather-man declared that this is the most cold season the country has had in a decade.

    A. this is the coldest eason the
    B. this has been the highest cold season the
    C. this was the coldest season the
    D. this is noted as the worst cold season the

32. Identify the correct version of the following sentence: As a result of his beautiful notation that still prevails, Mozart has been known as one of the most prolific music composers.

    A. has been known as the most
    B. had been known as the most
    C. was being known as the most
    D. is being seen as the most

33. **State the correct verb form:**

    Fill in the blank/blanks with the correct verb form: Politics — of greatest interest to most of us.

A. are

B. is

C. have been

D. should

34. Fill in the blank/blanks with the correct verb form: The teacher together with the students — in the bus.

    A. were

    B. are

    C. was

    D. have been

Math

1. What is the volume of an ice cube of width 7 inches?

    A. 434 cubic inches

    B. 343 cubic inches

    C. 21inches

    D. 257inches

2. We know that 1inch=2.54cms. A man is six feet tall. What do you think his approximate height would be in centimeters?

    A. 180 centimeters

    B. 184 centimeters

    C. 176 centimeters

    D. 158 centimeters

3. A room in your house is L yards long and W yards wide. What will be the cost of cleaning the room in dollars if the cleaners charge you 20 cents per square foot?

    A. $0.90LW

    B. $0.3LW

    C. $1.30LW

    D. $1.80LW

4. Martha bought three pieces of fabric to sew her quilt. The first fabric measured 3 yards 4 feet 2 inches in length, the second piece is 1 yard 4 feet 5 inches long, and the third piece was 5 yards 1 feet 4 inches in length. How much material has Martha bought to make the quilt?

    A. 10 yards 4 feet 5inches
    B. 12 yards 3 feet
    C. 12 yards 11inches
    D. 10 yards 5 feet 1inch

5. You have 500 milligrams of butter in your refrigerator. You need 368 milligram for the exact amount to bake a cake. How much of the butter will be left in the fridge?

    A. 232 grams
    B. .132milligrams
    C. 13.2grams
    D. 1.32grams

6. The measurements of a glass lobby are 12 feet✕10 feet✕8 feet. What is the volume of the lobby?

    A. 180 square feet
    B. 900 cubic feet
    C. 960 cubic feet
    D. 960 square feet

7. You went to buy some wool from the store to make a sweater. The storekeeper asks you the weight of the wool you need. Which of the following measurements must you mention to the storekeeper to get the requisite amount of wool?

    A. yards
    B. meters
    C. grams
    D. liters

8. One slice of a cake has 350 calories. What will be the calorie content of 3½ slices of the cake?

    A. 1050 calories
    B. 1750 calories
    C. 1250 calories
    D. 1500 calories

9. The perimeter of a rectangular shed is 54 yards. Its length is 32 feet. What is its width?

    A. 58feet
    B. 3 yards
    C. 49 feet
    D. 25 yards

10. Study the following picture, Which of the options given in the question represents the vertex of the angle?

    A. C
    B. D and E
    C. B
    D. A

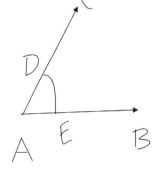

11. The diameter of a circle is 12. What is its approximate circumference?

    A. 36
    B. 48
    C. 60
    D. 24

12. What is the area of the triangle of height 6 cms, and base 12 cms drawn in the picture below?

    A. 44 square cms

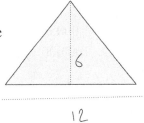

B. 28 square cms

C. 38 square cms

D. 36 square cms.

13. Study the geometrical figure given below. What is the measurement of the angle shown in the solid line?

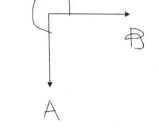

A. 360°

B. 270°

C. 180°

D. 90°

14. Look at the geometric figure; if angle A measures 145°, what is the measurement of angle B?

A. 25°

B. 35°

C. 45°

D. 55°

15. Which one of the following options is not equal to 10^5?

A. 100,000

B. 10×10×10×10×10

C. 10, 000

D. $10^3×10^2$

16. Multiply the following numbers.

$10^3×10^4$

A. 10^7

B. 10^{12}

C. 1,000,000

D. 100,000

17. What is the result of dividing a^6 by a^3?

    A. a^2
    B. a^3
    C. a^5
    D. a^9

18. An angle is 20° more than its complement. What is the measure of this angle?

    A. 45°
    B. 35°
    C. 55°
    D. 40°

19. You have been asked to find the measurement of an angle which is the complement of itself. What do you think the angle should measure?

    A. 90°
    B. 50°
    C. 25°
    D. 45°

20. The triangle ABC is an isosceles triangle, where the angle ABC is equal to angle ACB. AB is of length 6x–8, AC is 4x+2, and BC is of length 2x+2. You are required to find the value of x.

    A. 8
    B. 5
    C. 6
    D. 10

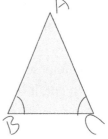

21. What is the measurement of angle B and angle C in this isosceles triangle? The measurement of angle A is 50°.

    A. 55°
    B. 65°
    C. 30°
    D. 45°

22. Three sides of a triangle are 6 centimeters, 8 centimeters, and 9 centimeters. What do you think is the nature of the triangle?

    A. it is an acute-angled triangle
    B. it is an obtuse-angled triangle
    C. it is a right-angled triangle
    D. the nature cannot be discerned.

23. In a right-angled triangle, the two sides are 5 centimeters and 12 centimeters. What should be the length of the hypotenuse?

    A. 14cms
    B. 10cms
    C. 13cms
    D. 15.5cms

24. In a right-angled triangle, the two sides are 5 centimeters and 12 centimeters, where the height (h) is 5 centimeters, and the triangle's base (b) is 12 centimeters. What is the area (A) of the right-angled triangle?

    A. 50 square centimeters
    B. 120 square centimeters
    C. 80 square centimeters
    D. 30 square centimeters

25. Suppose you have bought a share for $6.05. After twenty years of careful investment, it increases exponentially by 10^6 . What amount of return do you get from your investment?

    A. $60,500
    B. $605,000
    C. $605
    D. $6,050,000

26. You have a check for $780,000. Can you express this as an exponent of ten?

    A. 7.8×103

B. 7.8×104
C. 7.8×105
D. 78.00×102

27. 0.000764 is equal to one of the following options. Which, according to you, is the right choice?

A. 76.4×10-3
B. 76.4×10-4
C. 7.64×10-4
D. 764×10-5

28. Which of the fractions exists between ⅔ and ⅗ ?

A. ⅖
B. 1/15
C. ⅓
D. 31/50

29. Which of the following fractions is greater than 1/3 and less than ⅞?

A. ¼
B. 11/12
C. 23/24
D. 17/24

30. Their mother told Mary and Sam that Mary could have the square root of four pieces of a cake which must be less than two times Sam's number. Given that their mother wanted to test her children's math proficiency, what do you think was the number of pieces of cakes that Mary ate, if Sam had 20 pieces?

A. 10
B. 6
C. 8
D. 4

31. You are baking a cake. The recipe mentions 2⅔ cups of flour. Which fraction is this amount equivalent to?

    A. ³⁄₂
    B. ⅔
    C. ⁴⁄₃
    D. ⁸⁄₃

32. Sally kept stamps in her box. She had a collection of stamps from four different years. She had 20 stamps from the year 1887, 30 stamps from 1888, 40 stamps from 1889, and 10 stamps from 1890. You wanted to see a stamp from her collection. Sally reached into her box without looking and picked one up for you. What is the probability that she picked a stamp from the year 1887?

    A. 1/10
    B. ⅕
    C. ⅖
    D. 4/5

33. There are 39 candies in a box. You have to divide it equally between 9 children. Which of the following best resembles the number of candies each child will get?

    A. 4 candies
    B. 4⅓ candies
    C. 5 candies
    D. 4⅔ candies

34. Marie uses six ⅐ cups of sugar in a recipe. How many cups of sugar has she used?

    A. 10/7
    B. 3⁴⁄₇
    C. 46/7
    D. 3³⁄₇

Answer Key

Reading

Q	A	Q	A
1	i)A ii) A iii) A iv) A	18	C
2	B	19	C
3	D	20	D
4	D	21	B
5	C	22	D
6	B	23	A
7	C	24	B
8	D	25	A
9	D	26	D
10	D	27	B
11	C	28	D
12	A	29	B
13	B	30	B
14	C	31	C
15	A	32	A
16	C	33	D
17	B	34	B

Writing

Q	A	Q	A
1	B	18	B
2	B	19	C
3	C	20	C
4	D	21	A
5	C	22	D
6	C	23	C
7	A	24	D
8	B	25	I) C II) D III) A IV) C
9	D	26	D
10	D	27	D
11	D	28	C
12	D	29	D
13	D	30	A
14	C	31	A
15	B	32	D
16	A	33	B
17	C	34	C

Math

Q	1	2	3	4	5	6	7	8	9	10	11	12	13	14
A	B	A	D	C	B	C	C	B	C	D	A	D	B	B

Q	15	16	17	18	19	20	21	22	23	24	25	26	27	28
A	C	A	B	C	D	B	B	A	C	D	D	C	C	D

Q	29	30	31	32	33	34
A	D	B	D	C	B	D

Answer Key and Explanations

Reading

1. **i) A**

   ii) A

   iii) A

   iv) A

   All the words express an opinion and not fact.

2. **B**

   eclectic

   The word eclectic means a diverse choice, apt for the sentence.

3. **D**

   Although substantial also means important and concrete, in this context, choice d), grand is more apt.

4. **D**

   Aural means related to ears.

5. **C**

   profuse

6. **B**

   inattentive

You should always refer to the context to comprehend the meaning of a word.

7. **C**

give information

8. **D**

Although "protect" seems an enticing choice, the National Parks cannot protect their inhabitants from natural and man-made calamities. It does foster the growth of diverse flora and fauna.

9. **D**

Vertebrates are animals with vertebra, the supporting backbone. All the options mentioned have one.

10. **D**

The author mentions "vertebrates" in the line before.

11. **C**

Endangered means in danger of being attacked, compromised, or facing extinction.

12. **A**

The author is not referring to all the animal species of the parks, but only to the invertebrates and so, C is incorrect; the author is not talking about all the invertebrates of the world D.

13. **B**

We do not want a synonym for the word chaparral. A thesaurus will not serve our purpose. We do not know if the passage is from a book that comes with a glossary. An encyclopedia explains things while a dictionary explains the words. Dictionaries give information about the word you are looking up. An encyclopedia explores more details about those words, and, hence, the word may have a different entry name in the encyclopedia. For instance, chaparral may come under the section of a shrubland plant community.

14. **C**

In this context, breed means to beget offspring, and winter means to find shelter for the winter months. Many animals hibernate during the harsh winter months, and birds are known to migrate to warmer climates.

15. **A**

The text tells us about what Maynor found in her research work. It does not present a contrast between the two theories.

16. **C**

None of the options are true, except C. The style of e-mails is more informal.

17. **B**

The spellings can be found in other uses of language and are not characteristic of e-mails. The text does not mention the use of clipped words as problematic. Use of such an informal style is a feature of e-mails.

18. **C**

Expound means to explain.

19. **C**

Dissect in this context means to analyze.

20. **D**

Countenance means facial expression.

21. **B**

Countenance means facial expression.

22. **D**

"did" is a fact, the rest are opinions.

23. **A**

Only "always" is a fact; the rest are opinions. Note, intelligence is a fact, but intelligent is opinion.

24. **B**

Uncanny is the closest in meaning

25. **A**

The whole text describes the peculiar mental attribute of President Johnson; hence A is the only viable option.

The text is an opinion of the author, not corroborated by anyone else. President Johnson liked to tell the story of his intuitive power and not the author. There is no comparison between statements in the text.

26. **D**

Blood is not pronounced as 'oo' but rhymes with short 'u' as in umbrella.

27. **B**

mal is the root word which means bad.

28. **D**

Confinement has the Latin root word finis or fin, which means end or limit.

29. **B**

The root word is the basic word form with no prefixes or suffixes attached. "Phrase" is the basic form from which rephrased is derived. Phrased could also have been the answer, but a suffix -ed is attached to it, which automatically negates its qualification to become the root word.

30. **B**

Only hurt and sore are synonymous, feel means to examine through the sense of touch or to experience an emotion or sensation. Felt means to have considered, achieved, or attained. Come and go are antonyms. New and knew are homophones. Prise is a verb meaning opening something forcibly. On the other hand, a prize is a reward given to the competition winner.

31. **C**

Muster in this context means gathered.

32. **A**

It is obvious from the text that muster must mean gathering a crowd. Do not get confused by archaic and unfamiliar words. Read the passage well, paraphrase it, and get the text's main idea and purpose to understand the inherent meaning.

33. **D**

justified is the past tense of "justify."

34. **B**

The student probably did not understand the word chronologically or did not follow the directions carefully. Since the text does not discuss which events are most important, choice A is inappropriate. The text does not support other options.

Writing

1. **B**

"yet" is either a conjunction or an adverb. As a conjunction, it connects grammatically similar things like two words, phrases, or two clauses.

2. **B**

Prewriting is the brainstorming session when you plan what you are going to say about the subject. In the revising stage, you are evaluating the writing content. You check for coherence and whether you cited adequate examples. You look for effective transitions and clarity in the text you have written.

Editing is the stage where you evaluate the mechanical errors, which cannot take place until the content is well-written. Publishing is the final stage when the book is shared with a larger audience.

3. **C**

Moreover is the wrong choice of word for this sentence. Moreover is used to give some additional information or to connect a sentence to an already written related sentence. Like "additionally" and "besides," moreover is often used to begin a sentence.

4. **D**

Opened on and the East River.

5. **C**

either C or D is correct. C is definitely more appropriate and incontestable.

6. **C**

After you finish writing, you revise the text.

7. **A**

But is a coordinating conjunction, and a comma and not a semicolon should have preceded it.

8. **B**

The Modern Language Association (MLA) mentions that you should capitalize all nouns, pronouns, adjectives, verbs, adverbs, and subordinating conjunctions in a title. Articles. prepositions, and coordinating conjunctions should not be capitalized, nor the "to" in infinitives.

9. **D**

When comparing two things, use words like more, better, kinder, slower, etc. If, however, the comparison is among more objects, then you should use superlative degrees like most, best, kindest, slowest, etc. An easy way to remember this is to count the number of letters in the suffix that are added to the word to make a comparative or superlative degree. In most cases, you form a comparative degree by adding the suffix -er to the word. A superlative degree, on the other hand, takes the suffix -est. In the first case, you add only two words, thus corresponding to a difference between two things. In the latter instance, you need to add three words to show the comparison between things more than two.

In the question, since the comparison was between two babies (twins), you should use a comparative and not superlative degree.

10. **D**

Everywhere is an adverb of place.

11. **D**

Calendar

12. **D**

You should be alert for such words as *better, best, most, main/mainly, major,* and *primary/primarily* used in the questions. They indicate that other answers could be true, and you have to choose the *best* option among them.

13. **D**

doesn't

14. **C**

World **S**eries

15. **B**

The correct preposition in this sentence is "on."

16. **A**

Only "Multidisciplinary" has the correct spelling. Etiquette, Fulfillment, and Accommodation are spelled wrong.

17. **C**

Sam is thinking; hence he is the subject. A is a pronoun, B is an object, and D is a verb.

18. **B**

There is a wrong use of the verb. While expression can both be used as a countable and uncountable noun, its use in this sentence refers to a single concept.

19. **C**

it's and not its

20. **C**

The mnemonic for coordinating conjunction is FANBOYS: For, And, Nor, But, Or, Yet, and So.

For is mainly used as a preposition, though. For example, I bought this book *for* you.

21. **A**

Inundated means flooded with calls. Superseded means to take over a position, role, or place. Chastened means to be punished for some wrongdoing, and dispossessed means subjected to deprivation. Only inundated fits with the context of the sentence.

22. **D**

Gaffe means a mistake, reticent means shy. These two words fit in with the meaning of the sentence.

23. **C**

You should put a comma before giving and a semicolon before hence.

24. **D**

Adapt, maintenance

25. **i) C**

The sentence contains three or more words, phrases, or clauses. Consider inserting a comma to separate the elements.

The "serial comma" (the Oxford comma) is the last comma before coordinating conjunction and the final item in a series. Its use is considered a matter of style. Many style guides require the serial comma and a few advise against it. There are times, however, when you must use it to avoid confusion or ambiguity and for consistency. An example is,

Incorrect: "Make sure to pack sunscreens, towels, changes, sunglasses etc."

Correct: "Make sure to pack sunscreens, towels, changes, sunglasses, etc."

ii) D

We use a comma between two consecutive adjectives modifying the same noun. A comma between a verb and an object is the wrong usage. There should be no comma between an adjective and the noun it is modifying.

iii) A

There should be a comma both before and after Neil. When addressing someone by name, and it is in the middle of a sentence, in this case, between the subject and the object, you should set it off by commas on both sides. There should be no comma between auxiliary verb and verb **B**. No commas to set off the "inserted name" in a sentence is wrong C. Since there is an error in the sentence, **D** is wrong.

iv) C

A comma must be used between the street address, city, and state name. No comma should be used between the verb, and prepositional phrase (**B**), a comma between the subject and the predicate is not required (**A**). Since there is an error in the sentence, (**D**) is wrong

26. **D**

You should set off the modifying phrase between the subject and the predicate by placing a dash on both sides and not just putting a single dash. Non-matching punctuation marks, like a dash before and a comma after it, or a dash before and a colon after the word, are incorrect usages.

27. **D**

No one's is a possessive pronoun, and you have to put an apostrophe before s. No one is two words and not one (**b**), and it is not hyphenated.

28. **C**

The correct verb should be "were lying." Laying implies putting things down gently, and carefully. When you put something down in the proper position to use it, you use "laying."

29. **D**

The past unreal conditional should have "if" and the past perfect of the verb to read. Use the auxiliary verb "had" along with read. Would, should, or could is incorrect. In "if…then" past unreal usage, "would have" is always used in the second clause, which should have been set off with "then" and never in the first clause with "if."

30. **A**

We always use "who" when talking about a person, and not that (b) or which (c). The past perfect continuous had been spurned, being unsuitable in this context. A simple past tense "was" relates to the historical event. We use past perfect continuous to denote an action that started in the past and continued in the past. The action should also end at a certain point in the past. In this sentence, we could have used past perfect continuous tense if the sentence talked about a timeline.

31. **A**

The superlative should be rainiest and not more rainy. Most superlative forms have the endings -est, like longest, farthest, etc. Sometimes adjectives take the superlative most, for instance, "I am most tired on Thursdays."

32. **D**

Present perfect tense **A** means the action is still present. Past perfect **B** means the action stopped before some point in the past. Known is less accurate than seen. The former implies fact, and the latter suggests views, opinions, and perceptions, which is the case here. Was being— the past participle of the verb be is used to denote a continuous action in the past. **D** is the most appropriate sentence.

33. **B**

Politics as a science or study takes a singular form. It can be used in a plural sense in day-to-day conversations. For example, "My politics are my choice."

34. **C**

The sentence refers to the teacher and the students together; the correct choice of verb should be in the singular.

Math

1. **B**

The volume of a cube is expressed by the equation, $V=s3$, where V=volume and s=side. In the given sum, the width of the IceCube is 7 inches. A cube has the same measurements for length, breadth, and width. Therefore, the volume of the ice cube is 73, or 7×7×7=343 cubic inches.

2. **A**

In this sum, first, we need to convert six feet into inches. 6 feet is 6×12=72 inches. Therefore, the man's height in centimeters will be 72×2.54=182.88 inches. In the absence of a calculator, you can only take an approximate guess at the man's height in centimeters. You can multiply 72 by 2=144cms. Then multiply 72 by 0.5=36 centimeters. Add 36 and 144 centimeters; the result is 180 centimeters.

Always be careful of the unit of measurement that has been asked of you and the unit that is given in the sum.

3. **D**

In this sum, first, you must convert the area of the room in square feet from the square yard. The area of the room in square yards is given by the equation, A=L×W, or, LW square yards=9LW square feet. We calculated this because 1 yard=3feet.

The cost of cleaning your home in cents would be 20×9=180 cents=$1.80

Therefore, the cost of cleaning your room will be $1.80LW

4. **C**

You must convert each of the measurements into a single unit of measurement before you proceed any further with the sum.

i) 3 yards 4 feet 2 inches: Convert 3 yards to feet= 9 feet. 9+4=13feet=13×12inches=156inches' 156inches+2inches=158inches

ii) 1 yard 4 feet 5 inches=7feet 5inches= 84inches+5inches=89inches.

iii) 5 yards 1 feet 4 inches=16 feet 4inches=192 inches(-1foot=12inches)+4inches=196inches.

Martha has 158+89+196=443inches of material with her.

Now you have to convert 443 inches in the yard because the options given are in yards. 443inches=36.92 feet

Or, 12.306 yards.=12 yards 0.92 feet (.306 yard=.306✕3=0.918feet)

Or, 12 yards 11inches (0.92✕12).

Therefore, C is the right choice. A =413inches, b)=468 inches, and d)=420 inches

5. **B**

1gram =1000 milligram. Therefore, 132 milligrams can be expressed as 132/1000=0.132gram.

6. **C**

The volume of a rectangular prism is the product of length, width, and height. Therefore the volume of the glass lobby is 960 cubic feet. Volume is always expressed in the cubic feet; the area is expressed in square feet.

7. **C**

Weight is indicated by units grams, kilograms, or pounds and ounces.

8. **B**

Three slices of the cake have 350✕3=1050 calories. The ½ slice has 175 calories in it. Therefore, 3½ of this cake contains 1750 calories.

9. **C**

The perimeter of a rectangular structure is P=2L+2W, where P=perimeter, L=Length, and W=width.

54 yards=162feet.

162=2✕32 (L)+2W

Or, 162=64+2W

Or, 2W=98

Therefore, W=49

The width of the shed is 49feet.

10. **D**

The vertex is always formed by the two rays of an angle meeting at a point which is A in the picture.

11. **A**

The circumference of a circle C=πd, where π is a constant of value 3.14, and d=the diameter of the circle.

Replacing the values in the equation, we can write the equation as follows:

C=3.14×12

Or, C=37.68

However, the question asks you to suggest an approximation. Of all the choices that are given to you as a possible answer to the question, 36 is definitely the most appropriate choice.

12. **D**

From the picture of the triangle, we know that the height of the triangle is 6 cms, and the base is 12 cm. The equation for the area A of the triangle is=½ bh, where b=base and h= height.

A= ½ *6*12

A=36 square cms.

13. **B**

We know that when two rays are perpendicular to each other, they form 90°. When they meet at a straight line, forming a straight angle, the angle measures 180°. The measurement of the angles increases after this. The angle formed by the meeting of two rays is now called a "Reflex angle."

A Reflex angle is always more than 180°, but less than 360°.

When the rays meet each other in the way shown in the figure, the angle formed is 180°+90°=270°. Ray A has moved perpendicular to Ray B but goes in the lower quadrant instead of the upper.

Another way to do the sum is to take away 90° from the sum of all angles formed by two perpendicular rays, that is 360°. Therefore, the value is 360°−90° =270°

14. **B**

The full measurement of the angle formed by the two rays is 180° (straight angle). If angle A measures 145°, angle B measures 180−145=35°

15. **C**

All of the options are the same as 10^5, except 10,000. It has four zeroes in it which can be written as 10^4

16. **A**

Other options are invalid because they do not have an appropriate number of zeroes. When you are multiplying two same bases, their exponents are added. $10^{3+4}=10^7$

17. **B**

Although A seems an enticing option, it would be a wrong choice. When two same bases have different exponents, their division is equal to the subtraction between the exponents. $a^6/a^3 = a^{6-3}$.

Or, a^3.

18. **C**

When the sum of two angles is 90°, they are called complementary.

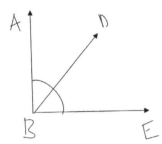

The angle indicated in the solid line is the sum of two smaller angles, ABD and angle DBE. They are complementary angles because they together form the right angle that measures 90°.

In this sum, let us consider that the angle to be measured is "a." the complementary angle should measure $(90-a)°$.

According to the criteria given to us, we may write $(90-a)° = a°-20$

Or, $90+20=2a$.

We may rewrite this as,

$2a=110$

Or, $a=55$

The other angle should measure $90-55=35°$

But the question has asked us the measure of angle a, which is $55°$

19. **D**

This question tells us that the angle is a complement of itself. Since complementary angles sum up to 90°, each of them should measure 45° to be the exact complement of each other.

To solve the sum, we may write

a+a =90°, because both the angles have the same measurement.

Or, 2a=90°

Or, a=45°

20. **B**

An isosceles triangle has two equal sides, AB and AC. They are called the "legs" of an isosceles triangle. The remaining side, BC, is called the "Base." Since the two legs of an isosceles triangle are congruent, angle B= angle C.

In this sum, we may write the equation as

6x–8=4x+2 since the two legs are the same.

Or, 6x-4x=2+8

Or, 2x=10

Therefore, x=5.

21. **B**

We know that AB is equal to AC (they are the legs of an isosceles triangle).

And, angle B= angle C

The sum of all angles of an isosceles triangle is always 180°. The sum tells us that angle A is 50°.

For an isosceles triangle, Angle A+Angle B + Angle C=180°.

We know that Angle A= Angle B because they are congruent angles. Let us consider they measure x, where x is the variable.

Therefore, x+x+50=180

Or, 2x=180–50
Or, 2x= 130
Or, x=65

Therefore, both the angles B and C measure 65°

22. **A**

Let us review what an acute-angled triangle is. According to the Pythagoras theorem, an Acute-angled triangle has the *square of the longest side* **less** than the *sum of the squares of two smaller sides*.

Let us consider 'a', 'b', and 'c' are the length of sides of the triangle in question; in which side 'a' is the longest, then according to the theorem, we may say the given triangle is acutely angled if a2 < b2 + c2.

In this case, the longest dimension is 9 centimeters.

$9^2 < 6^2 + 8^2$

Or, 81<36+64

Or, 81<100, which is true.

The triangle is, therefore, an acute-angled triangle.

23. **C**

We know that the hypotenuse is the side opposite to the right angle, and it is the longest side of a right-angled triangle.

Let us now consider the sides of this triangle as a, b, and c, where c is the hypotenuse. Then using the Pythagorean formula, we may write

$a^2 + b^2 = c^2$.

Or, $5^2+12^2=c^2$

Or, $25+144=c^2$

We may rewrite this as, $c^2=369$

Or, c=13 centimeters.

24. **D**

We know that in a right-angled triangle, the base and the height are the two sides that form the right angle. Multiplying these two values together would give the area of the corresponding rectangle, and the right-angled triangle is half of that; therefore, we may write the formula as

Area (A) of the triangle= ½*base*height

Or, ½*12*5

Or, A=30 square

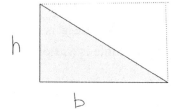

25. **D**

6.05×10^6 =?

The decimal should be moved to the right to six places. Therefore, there will be four zeroes after 605.

26. **C**

Move the decimal to the right of the digit 7; you get the equivalent expression of 7.8×10^5, because there are five digits to the right of 7.

27. **C**

You may take the help of a number line to solve the problem.

Begin by marking on the number line the decimal point to the right of the one. The decimal point separates whole number values on the left from the fractional values on the right.

I have tried to draw a crude diagram to facilitate your understanding of the decimal placement on the number line. As you move to the right from the decimal d, the value decreases by a tenth, hundredth, and thousandth of the number. On the other hand, when you move to the left, the values are tens, hundreds, thousands, and so on.

As you move from left to right along with the decimal place-value system, you need to **divide** by ten each time you move. Continue this dividing process to the right of the decimal point to get the rest of the decimal system.

You will have to move **the decimal** to the right of the 7. You get a number that is equivalent to 7.64×10^{-4}.

The decimal needs to be moved by four places to the right to give the number.

28. **D**

We can solve this sum by converting the fraction into its decimal values.

Thus, ⅔ = 0.666, and ⅗ =0.6

Now, let us try to solve the answers to find out the fraction which lies in between 0.66 and 0.6.

⅖ =0.4

1/15= 0.066

⅓= 0.33

and 31/50=0.62

It is obvious that 0.62 lies in between the values 0.6 and 0.66. Therefore, 31/50 is your answer.

29. **D**

We can solve this sum by converting the fraction into its decimal values.

Thus, ⅓=0.333, ⅞ =0.875.

Now, let us try to solve the answers to find out the fraction which is greater than 0.33 and less than 0.875.

¼=0.25

11/12= 0.916

23/24= 0.958

and, 17/24= 0.708

Only 0.708 is more than 0.33, and less than 0.875.

It is clear that the last fraction 17/24 is more than ⅓ but less than ⅞.

30. **B**

Let us consider that Sam had x pieces of the cake. We can then write Mary's share as 2x-4. Let us now substitute x with the number provided, 8. We may now write the equation as 2(20)-4, or 36. Now we must simplify the number, which will give us 6. Therefore, Mary had 6 pieces of the cake.

You may also solve the sum by a little back-calculation. If Mary's portion must be a square root of four less than two times Sam's share, Sam's share should be first multiplied by 2, that is 40, and then 4 (which is 2 squared) subtracted from it. The remaining is 36, which when squared (as Mary's mother suggested) is 6.

31. **D**

The value of 2 is equivalent to 6/3. Therefore, 2⅔ can be written as 6/3 +⅔ = (6+2)/3=8/3. There is another way to find the answer. 2⅔= (3*2+2)/3 =(6+2)/3=8/3

32. **C**

You can add all the stamps that Sally had in her box. They sum up to 100. She had 20 stamps from the year 1887. Therefore, the probability that she would pick up a stamp from that year is 20 out of 100, or 20/100 or, ⅕.

33. **B**

The question asks to divide 39 candies **equally** among 9 children. 39/9= 4 3/9 or 4⅓

34. **D**

Six $^4/_7$ cups of sugar= the product of 6 and 4/7. This is equivalent to 24/7, since this is an improper fraction, we can write it as $3^3/_7$.

Practice Test #3

Reading

Read the following paragraph and then answer questions 1 and 2.

They first saw Richard The Lionheart from a distance, but even then, he was a sight that took their breath away. His red beard flickered like a flame. His eyes flashed with the radiance of stars. His breastplate glowed like molten silver. His disarming smile was like the morning sun that greets when one throws open the windows. Here was a man anyone would follow. He was a man who led.

1. Your students are studying how this text uses comparisons to describe the knight. You, as a paraprofessional, ask the students what the comparisons have in common.

    Which of the following answers is most appropriate?

    A. All of the comparisons mention light.
    B. All the comparisons refer to some sort of metal.
    C. All comparisons use the term "like."
    D. All comparisons are about the knight's face.

2. What question should you ask your students as a paraprofessional to help them understand the observers' viewpoint toward the knight?

    A. What were the observers doing before meeting the knight?
    B. How does the sight of the knight affect the observers?
    C. Why should the observer throw open the windows?
    D. When did the observer first see the knight?

3. You asked your students to think up pairs of synonymous words. Four such pairs of words are given below. Which is a pair of synonyms?

    A. Fell and fail
    B. Past and present
    C. Rain and weather
    D. Flush and level

4. Your students have learned that the letter "c" can sometimes sound like the letter "s." You have told them to find instances when this happens. They worked out several examples. Which of the following words from the story is the best example of how "c" can sound like "s"?

    "I was walking the trail when the peals of a cymbal attracted me. I was curious. Walking a little ahead, I chanced upon a church; its beauty and simplicity captivated me."

    A. captivate
    B. attracted
    C. church
    D. curious
    E. cymbal

Read the following story and then answer the next two questions that are based on it.

Bea's Balloon Ride

Chapter 1: A Birthday Surprise for Bea

"I'm six!" Bea shouted as soon as she woke up on Sunday morning. She ran to wake her parents, who were already up, as excited as Bea was. "I'm six," She said as she came down to the kitchen to meet her parents. Dad was at the table sipping coffee. He said, "You sure are." Her mom was making pancakes. She flipped a pancake and said, "You're getting so big."

When Bea finished breakfast, her father said, "We have a surprise for you."

"The circus?" Bea asked. She knew there was a circus in town, and she wished to see it.

"No," her mom said, "That will be another time."

"Where then?" Asked Bea.

"It's a surprise," her parents cried as they all got in the car.

The journey took quite some time. At last, Bea spotted a sign that said, "Michael's Airfield." Then she looked up in the sky and gasped at the most amazing sight floating in the air.

5.

i) Where did Bea find her parents? Which answer is most appropriate?

A. In her room
B. In her parents' room
C. In the kitchen
D. Downstairs

ii) You are guiding students who are learning how to make predictions about a story by using clues from the title of the story, the chapter headings, and what happens within the story. You ask the students, "What do you think Bea's surprise will be?"

Which answer shows that the student has the best understanding of the clues?

A. An helicopter ride
B. An elephant in midair
C. A balloon ride

D. A visit to McDonalds'.

6. Your students learned compound words consisting of more than one whole word joined together. Which of the following words is a compound word?

   A. comeback
   B. enterprise
   C. acknowledgment
   D. backtalk

7. *We should get effective political <u>pushback</u> against Hollywood's authoritarianism on copyrights.*

   In this sentence, what do you think is the meaning of the word "pushback?"

   A. grip
   B. strike
   C. cling to
   D. welcome

8. In this sentence, what do you think is closest in meaning to the word "supine?"

   She was lying supine on the beach.

   A. assertive
   B. prone
   C. vertical
   D. horizontal

9. *Sam's proclivity for cynicism makes him very unpopular among his friends.*

   Which word is closest in meaning to "proclivity?"

   A. penchant
   B. hatred
   C. unwillingness
   D. disregard

Read the following text and then answer the next questions.

Oppositional Defiant Behavior

Have you been irritable on any day and considered it your bad day? Have you used harsh tones with your teachers and parents or verbally disrespected them? We all have a short temper at times, but the current figures show that 16%–20% of school children have a psychological disorder called Oppositional Defiant Behavior.

It includes difficulty in obeying instructions or being pliant with requests; they engage in unnecessary arguments with adults, throw temper tantrums, and have difficulty in accepting responsibility for their actions. They get easily frustrated and show annoying behaviors. Parents feel that a relationship with ODD is like moving from conflict to conflict.

It can be due to child neglect, abuse, trauma, or a reaction to severe disciplinary actions taken at home. Some of the families have a history of mood disorders or family history of violence.

Various therapies are available to treat ODD, and some drugs can be prescribed. No single cure exists. Psychologists believe that the best advice is given to the parents to help their children.

10. In the above text, what do you think is the author's purpose?

    A. scare one away from ODD
    B. ODD children can be victims of childhood trauma.
    C. Frustration about ODD
    D. It is a fact that the parents are to blame for ODD in children.

11.

    A. ODD children are destined to turn out delinquent.
    B. Parents are not responsible for their ODD children
    C. ODD can be treated.
    D. No cure exists for ODD.

Read the following text, a discussion, and then answer questions 12-18 based on the topic.

"Native Speaker" by Chang-Rae Lee is an award-winning debut novel about a man named Henry Park, a Korean-American individual who struggled to find his identity as an immigrant to America. He lived in the suburbs of New York City. The novel addresses the concept that the individuals who know us best, like our family, peers, and partners, are the ones who give sense and direction to our lives and ultimately define us.

The novel starts with a cryptic line: The day my wife left, she gave me a list of who I was.

Throughout the novel, Park, who worked as a sleuth, struggled with racial and ethnic identity crises triggered by his loneliness. This dual reality of existence as a sleuth working for America and an unwelcome immigrant increased his sense of confusion concerning his position in society. He felt like a constant outsider, looking in from the outside. He believed that he belonged to neither world.

Chang-Rae Lee is himself a first-generation Korean-American immigrant. Lee is also the author of "A Gesture Life" and "A Loft." His parents emigrated to America when Chang-Rae was three. Recurrent themes of identity, race and cultural conflicts permeate his works. His interests in them undoubtedly emanate from his experience growing up in a Korean household while attending an American school. The protagonists in all his books are similar. They deal with identifications based on race, color, and language. Consequently, all of these characters struggle to belong. The author urges us to think about the role of borders and why we are so scared of the idea of opening up one's borders. In an unpredictable world, cultures are increasingly becoming intermingled, and there is a constant urge to redefine the meaning of identity, especially when the security of belonging to a place becomes more ambiguous.

12. Who was Henry Park?

    A. The protagonist
    B. The author
    C. The deserter
    D. The wife-beater

13. What does the author think we should be concerned about?

    A. Immigrants are destroying national integrity.
    B. Immigrants should be banned from America.
    C. Immigrants should be welcomed without reservations.
    D. The problems the immigrants face are very relevant to the current geopolitical conditions.

14. Why do you think the author of the text started with the particular quote about Park's wife?

    A. It is a theme of the novel
    B. To rudely shock the readers
    C. To assert the novel is semi-biographical
    D. To create reader's interest
    E. It is the central idea of the novel.

15. Which of the following best describes the author's intention about the discussion?

    A. he wanted to criticize Chang-Rae Lee.
    B. he wanted to sympathize with the author
    C. he wanted to inform us about immigrants
    D. he wanted to analyze the situation

16. According to the author of the passage, Chang-Rae's interest in writing novels stemmed from certain events. Which of the following do you think mainly motivated him to write?

    A. War in Korea
    B. Bullying at an American school.
    C. School Essay contest for international students.
    D. Conflicting living conditions during his childhood in America

17. The author of the passage mentions that all the characters of Chang-Rae's novels are similar. What, according to the text, do they refer to?

    A. All his characters are male

B. All his characters are immigrants
C. His characters don't know English.
D. His characters fight for identity.

18. What, according to you, does the author of the passage feel strongly about?

    A. Border issues
    B. Racial harmony
    C. Identity crises of the immigrants in an ever-changing and intermingling world.
    D. Identity crises of everyone in an ever-changing and intermingling world.

Read the next passage carefully and then answer questions 19-23.

The government needs to select from a comprehensive menu of regulatory approaches when it decides to curb emissions. One of the choices can be direct control, which will involve setting emissions standards for implements and procedures, requiring domestic and factories to use standardized equipment, or prohibiting them from using those other than the ones prescribed. Alternately, the government can approach indirectly by encouraging incentive-based tactics, offering them either singly or in combination. For instance, the government could restrict overall quantities of emissions through a system of permits. It can also impose taxes or fees on higher grades of emissions. Conversely, those who will pollute less will pay less. Incentive-based approaches are usually less costly than direct controls to regulate greenhouse gas emissions.

19. In the text, what do you think is the meaning of incentive-based?

    A. Letting people know the punishment they will get for not obeying.
    B. Convincing others to change their behavior by promising rewards.
    C. Everyone should comply.
    D. Adopting research-based methods.

20. The construction of the text is one of the following.

    A. Cause-effect analysis
    B. Explaining back-to-back on the know-how of things.
    C. Describing the options
    D. Comparing two conflicting concepts.

21. What, according to you, is the main purpose of the text?

    A. To alert the government about the hazards of Greenhouse emissions.
    B. To persuade the readers that they should reduce Greenhouse gases
    C. To give the writer's opinion on the most effective way to control Greenhouse emissions.
    D. To tell the readers the different ways the government can adopt to control emissions.

22. What idea do you get from the last sentence of the text?

    "Incentive-based approaches are usually less costly than direct controls to regulate greenhouse gas emissions."

    A. Greenhouse gases are causing climate change.
    B. Direct emission control methods for Greenhouse gases are costly.
    C. Incentive-based emission control is a smart option.
    D. At present, there are no rules on emission control.

23. What is closest in meaning to the term "cost-effective?"

    A. A return in benefit justifying the initial investment
    B. Using or expending without restrictions.
    C. Intending to impress.
    D. Of the best quality.

Look at the following pictogram and then answer questions 24-28.

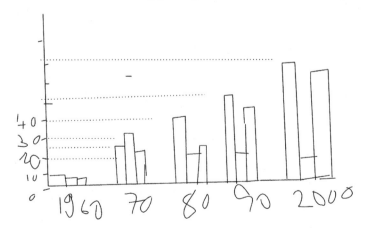

In this crude diagram, the vertical axis represents the percentage of items recycled. Each mark denotes, 0%, 10%, 20%, 30% and so on. The bars on the horizontal axes represent paper, glass, and metals, respectively, from left to right. The years for recycles are mentioned.

24. What is the most recycled material?

    A. Paper
    B. Plastics
    C. Metals
    D. None of them

25. In which year was recycling approaching 10%?

    A. 2000
    B. 1980
    C. 1970
    D. 1960

26. Which conclusion can be safely derived from the picture of the chart?

    A. Recycling before 1960 was not an important concept.
    B. Recycling between 1970 and 1980 was absent.
    C. The chart shows no data to indicate the rate of recycling materials increased or decreased in 1960.
    D. Rate of recycling was affected worse in 1980 than in 1970.

27. Which of the following objects showed a comparative decline in recycling over the subsequent years?

    A. Paper
    B. Glass
    C. Metal
    D. None of these.

28. You have asked your students to alphabetize and define a list of five words. The words are: distinguish, acclimatize, conversational, banish, and introduce. How will you suggest they perform the task?

    A. The students will start by defining the words based on their existing knowledge of their own words and then position them in alphabetical order.
    B. They will start by alphabetizing the first letter of each word. If the first letters are the same, they will move to the second in succession. They will then use a dictionary to search for the meaning of the words to define them.
    C. Start alphabetizing the first letter of the words and then use the internet to check the synonyms for the words to define them.
    D. The students will define the words first by consulting a dictionary and then alphabetizing them according to the length of the word.

29. You are explaining to the students the proper method of prereading strategies the students should adopt to approach a text. Which of the following is *not* the correct method.

    A. Investigating the book cover to gain insights into the text.
    B. Preparing a list of all unfamiliar vocabulary words and consulting their meaning before reading the text.
    C. Browsing through the introduction of the text.
    D. Study the associated charts, diagrams, and pictures.

30. You are a paraprofessional. What question should you ask a student to make sure that they understand what they are supposed to do after reading a written direction for a task?

    A. Do they understand what they should do?
    B. Do the directions look consistent?
    C. What does the direction mean to the student?
    D. Do you have any questions about what you should do?

Read the following text and then answer questions 31 and 32.

Clara and Matthew decided to go to the grocery store for some flour and butter. Clara wanted to bake a cake for their son's upcoming birthday. When they entered the store, Matthew got a shopping basket for Clara. They filled their basket with flour, butter, milk, honey, chocolates, and birthday candles. Clara picked up a package of candies to enjoy returning home. Matthew discovered he was short of change at the checkout counter, and there was not enough money to buy all the items in their basket. They decided to put the candies back on the shelf.

31. What question should a paraprofessional ask their students about the text that would *best* help them to understand why Clara and Matthew put the candies back?

    A. Why Clara and Matthew did not bring more money or credit cards?
    B. How did they feel when they found they could not enjoy their candy back home?
    C. What did they go to buy at the store?
    D. Why did Clara not put back on the shelf an item other than the package of the candies?

32. "Matthew discovered he was short of change at the checkout counter, and there was not enough money to buy all the items in their basket."

    The word "change" means one of the following words in this sentence. Identify the word.

    A. amend
    B. switch
    C. vary
    D. money

33. You, as a paraprofessional, want to encourage the student to think of an antonym for the word change as has been used in the text. Which of these would be a correct antonym for the word change concerning the passage?

    A. preserve
    B. dollar
    C. penny
    D. keep

34. Which is *not* a proper strategy to build fluency in reading?

    A. You should use a tape recorder to assist the student with reading.

B. Assign another partner to read with the student.

C. The student should be involved in choral reading.

D. You should read out to the student unhurriedly and loudly.

Writing

1. Identify the correct grammar construction for the following sentence.

    Because he <u>had an</u> impressive memory, he has never forgotten a face.

    A. had an
    B. did have
    C. has
    D. has had

2. Identify the best grammar construction for the following sentence.

    "Many astrophysicists are still hoping <u>to have found</u> a solution for intergalactic travel."

    A. to have found
    B. to find
    C. to have been found
    D. of having found

3. Identify the correct grammar construction for the following sentence.

    "She has lain her cricket bat on the ground."

    A. has lain
    B. has laid
    C. have laid
    D. is lying

Identify the correct grammar construction for the following sentences from #4-#14.

4. Fiona consented to bring the present that she <u>bought in</u> the fair to the party.

    A. had bought in
    B. had bought at
    C. bought at
    D. did buy in

5. When night came, <u>and the temperature fell</u>, Abbott lit the fire in the living room.

    A. ,and the temperature fell,
    B. and when the temperature fell
    C. and because the temperature fell
    D. and that the temperature fell

6. Did she know that World Smile Day always <u>came on</u> the first Friday in October?

    A. came on
    B. comes on
    C. has come on
    D. had come on

7. Towering 4,207 meters above the sea level, Mauna Key <u>is an impressive site.</u>

    A. was an impressive site.
    B. makes an impressive site.
    C. is an impressive site
    D. is an impressive sight

8. At the moment, dictionaries come in a wide variety of forms, such as antonym and synonym dictionaries, biographical dictionaries, and geographical dictionaries <u>that has pronunciations given.</u>

    A. that include pronunciations.
    B. with pronunciations' included.
    C. that includes pronunciations.
    D. that has pronounciations given.

9. San Francisco <u>lays west</u> of Oakland.

    A. lies west
    B. is lying west
    C. lain west
    D. has laid west

10. The Titanic <u>sunk</u> on May 31, 1911, just four years before the Lusitania.

    A. was sunk
    B. had sunk
    C. sank
    D. sunk

11. <u>Has any of the</u> relatives been ushered in yet?

    A. Is any of the
    B. Are any of the
    C. Have any of the
    D. Has any of the

12. Neither of the Hurt sisters <u>expect to be selected in</u> the major basketball team this year.

    A. expect to be selected in
    B. is expecting to be selected for
    C. has expected to be selected in
    D. expects to be selected for

13. Identify the verb in the following sentence.

    When the Star Wars movie came to town, all the tickets <u>had sold out for</u> in advance.

    A. had sold out for
    B. had sold out far
    C. were sold out far
    D. had been sold out far

14. The origins of <u>existence is unknown</u>.

    A. existence are unknown
    B. existences are unknown
    C. existences have been unknown
    D. existence has been unknown

15. **Identify the noun in the following sentence.**

    i) The works of many great authors are placed on reserve.

    A. Many
    B. Great
    C. Reserve
    D. Placed

    ii) Shark and electric rays are not true fish; their skeletons are of cartilage and not bone.

    A. True
    B. Their
    C. Cartilage
    D. Not

    Identify the verb in the following sentences.

    iii) Sheila used to spell words backward.

    A. Words
    B. Backward
    C. used to
    D. Sheila

    iv) It is an atrocious disregard of diplomatic neutrality to infiltrate a foreign embassy.

    A. Infiltrate
    B. It

C. Atrocious

D. Neutrality

16. **Identify the verb in the following sentences.**

i) The wet papers <u>were spread</u> in sunlight.

A. wet

B. papers

C. spread

D. in

ii) The rash decision of the Trojans to receive the wooden horse brought their destruction.

A. Decision

B. Destruction

C. Receive

D. Rash

17. i) Identify the correct sentence from the given choices.

Sam said, "Mary didn't mentioned about a doberman pinscher dog."

A. "Mary didn't mention a Doberman pinscher dog."

B. "Mary doesn't mentioned about a Doberman Pinscher Dog".

C. Mary didn't mention about a doberman Pinscher Dog.

D. "Mary didn't mentioned about a doberman pinscher dog".

ii) Choose the correct word for the gap in the sentence below.

Rose is a voracious reader, very —in her taste.

A. incongruous

B. eclectic

C. superfluous

D. specific

18. Which of the following sentences does not use an apostrophe correctly?

    A. Disciplinary rules aren't easy to follow.
    B. The mouse caught its foot in a trap.
    C. Its difficult to see things from others' perspectives.
    D. Sheila's brother is four years older than her.

19. Which one of the following choices is appropriate for the sentence below?

    Ralph W. Emerson, the noted philosopher, wrote <u>in his work "Self-Reliance" of</u> the importance for an individual to sharpen his capacities.

    A. in his work, "Self-Reliance," of
    B. in his work; "Self-Reliance" about
    C. in his work: "Self-Reliance" of
    D. in his work "Self-Reliance" about

20. Which one of the following choices is appropriate for the sentence below?

    Her students just finished<u> reading— "Tales of the Grotesque and Arabesque,"</u> a book by Edgar Allan Poe.

    A. reading "Tales of the Grotesque and Arabesque—"
    B. reading, "Tales of the Grotesque and Arabesque,"
    C. reading "Tales of the Grotesque and Arabesque,"
    D. reading: "Tales of the Grotesque and Arabesque,"

21. Which one of the following choices is appropriate for the sentence below?

    In December we <u>will be married for thirty-five years</u>.

    A. will be married for thirty five year
    B. will have been married for thirty-five years
    C. will have married for thirty five years
    D. will be married for thirty-five years

22. Which one of the following choices is appropriate for the sentence below?

    The Diary of Anne Frank depicted a young girl's determination in the face of adversity.

    A. depicted a young girl's determination
    B. has depicted a young girl's determination
    C. depicts a young girl's determination
    D. depicted a young girls determination

23. Which one of the following choices is appropriate for the sentence below?

    The first portion of the examination is on mathematics, the second is on economics, and the third is on English.

    A. on mathematics, the second is on economics, and the third is on English.
    B. on mathematics, the second is on economics, and the third is on english.
    C. on mathematics, the second is on economics and the third is on English.
    D. on mathematics; the second is on economics, and the third is on English.

24. Which one of the following choices is appropriate for the sentence below?

    Among the many courses on arts, no matter what turns you on, there are several subjects to study.

    A. arts, no matter what turns you on,
    B. Arts, no matter what turns you on,
    C. Arts, no matter what you select,
    D. arts, no matter which you choose,

25. Which one of the following choices is appropriate for the sentence below?

    The word homologus is from Greek *homos* "same," and *logos* "proportion."

    A. *homos,* "same," and *logos,* "proportion."
    B. *homos* -"same," and *logos,* "proportion."
    C. *homos*- *"same,"* and *Logos* *"proportion."*

D. *homos-* same-, and logos -proportion.

26. Which one of the following choices is appropriate for the sentence below?

Seeing the dolphins, some eels, some jellyfish, and a killer whale made the visit to the marine park memorable.

A. some jelly fish, and a killer whale made the visit
B. some jellyfish, and a killer whale made the visit
C. some jelly fishes, and a killer whale make the visit
D. some jelly fish and a Killer whale makes the visit

27. Which one of the following choices is appropriate for the sentence below?

Yet, the fact that a planet is present outside the solar system kindles faith that other solar systems are there, and in them, probably, a planet that sustains life.

A. that a planet is present outside the solar system kindles faith that other solar systems are there and
B. that a planet is present outside the solar system kindles faith that other solar systems are there, and
C. maybe that a planet is present outside the solar system kindles faith that other solar systems are there, and
D. that a planet is present outside the solar system kindles faith that other solar systems is there, and

28. There are two underlined sections in the following sentence; pick the correct use of punctuation from the choices given below.

Online shopping can be time saving and handy with proper precautions, it is safe as well.

A. can be time-saving and handy, AND precautions, it is safe
B. should be time saving and handy AND precautions, it is safe
C. could be timesaving and handy; AND precautions; it is safe
D. can be time-saving and handy; AND precautions, it is safe

29. Each sentence has an error, or no error at all. But there is not more than one error per sentence. The error, if present, is underlined. Select the one underlined part that needs to be changed to make the sentence correct. If the sentence is correct select choice 5.

    The facts that (a) <u>Marie was given</u> by the three doctors (b) <u>make her understand</u> how much (c) <u>her mother's health</u> (d) <u>had deteriorated</u> (e) <u>no error</u>.

    A. a)
    B. b)
    C. c)
    D. d)
    E. e)

30. Stacy and her daughter Clara, (a) <u>neither</u> of (b) <u>whom</u> like sports (c) <u>is going</u> to see a film (d) <u>instead</u> (e) <u>no error</u>.

    A.
    B.
    C.
    D.

31. The audience (a) <u>is absorbed</u> for the (b) <u>duration</u> of the musical performance, and (c) <u>applaud</u> when the (d) <u>show ends</u> (e) <u>no error</u>.

    A.
    B.
    C.
    D.
    E.

32. Find the sentence with the misplaced modifier.

    A. Abraham Lincoln wrote the Gettysburg Address on the back of an envelope while traveling to Washington.
    B. Only after Laura has returned will we know what really happened.
    C. Stella and Laura wandered around the market for several pleasant hours.
    D. After descending through the clouds, London lay beneath us.

33. Find the nature of the error in the following sentences

   i) <u>The valet bring in</u> the car.

   ii) <u>The owners of the car is</u> happy.

   iii) Cars travel faster on Expressways than <u>on most other road</u>.

   iv) Which <u>of the following sentences do not use</u> the apostrophe correctly?

   A. Squinting modifier
   B. wrong preposition
   C. wrong use of articles
   D. wrong subject-verb agreement.

34. Identify the subject/subjects in the following sentence.

   Rose really liked the painting because it reminded her of her childhood."

   A. Rose and it
   B. painting
   C. It
   D. Rose

Math

1. Study the chart below carefully. The chart shows corresponding values for "b" against "a." What do you think should be the missing value for a?

a	b
1	1.5
2	3
	4.5
4	6
5	7.5
6	9

A. 2.5
B. 3
C. 4
D. 4.5

2. Bobby's Catering Company makes the best fruit salad using only four ingredients. They use five apples for every mango, three pears for every apple, and one pineapple for every mango. If they used five pineapples in their most recent batch, how many total pieces of fruit did they use?

A. 64
B. 72
C. 110
D. 100

3. Jill decides to change her present aquarium from a 20 liters aquarium to a 50 liters aquarium. She added 4 tablespoons of salt to her old aquarium. If she wishes to maintain the same salinity level, how many tablespoons should she add to her new aquarium?

A. 6 tablespoon
B. 10 tablespoon
C. 12 tablespoon
D. 8 tablespoon

4. At the end of a factory assembly line, completed nuggets have to be deposited into a box until it is filled. If, after 20 minutes, the box contains 25 nuggets and it takes 2 hours total to fill up a box, how many nuggets does a box hold?

A. 120
B. 125
C. 140
D. 150

5. Sarah and Bob have opened a fruit salad kiosk. Sarah tells Bob that she will pay him 1/5th of ½ of the profits earned, 3/5 of 2/3rd of the profit, 4/5th of ¾, or ⅘ th of ¼ of the profits. Bob is in a dilemma. Which offer do you think is the best one?

    A. The first offer
    B. The second offer
    C. The third offer
    D. The fourth offer.

6. In the above case, the best that Bob can earn from the fruit salad kiosk is which of the following?

    A. 1/10
    B. ⅖
    C. ⅗
    D. 1/2

7. Find the lowest common denominator for the fractions that are listed below for you.

    1/6, 1/8, and 2/10

    A. 100
    B. 80
    C. 120
    D. 60

8. In the following question, the algorithm given to you is a standard addition algorithm. It has three variables, a, b, and c. They each represent different values. You have to find out the value of the sum given.

    4a+27+b5 =c14

    A. 88
    B. 72
    C. 114
    D. 48

9. You have been asked to begin with the number 5, then add -3, and then subtract -5. What is the result you will have?

   A. 3
   B. 7
   C. -7
   D. -3

10. 1.5+6.44+19+25.52+42.55

    You are given a set of numbers and asked to find the difference between the sum of the set estimated to the nearest tenth value and then calculate the difference of the value from the exact sum. You found the difference to be one of the following.

    A. 0.12
    B. 1
    C. 0.01
    D. 10

11. Shon and James were playing a video game. Shon scored 149,750 points, while James scored 90,190 points. Which of the following estimates how many points Shon scored over James in the video game?

    A. 140,000
    B. 5,900
    C. 59000
    D. 59,600

12. 1.6+6.45+19+25.45+42.55

    You are given a set of numbers and asked to find the difference between the sum of the set estimated to the nearest tenth value and then calculate the difference of the value from the exact sum. You found the difference to be one of the following.

    A. 95.01
    B. 89
    C. 0.1
    D. .05

13. Alex regularly lifts weights at the gym. He can lift weights of 5.5 kg. What is 5.5kg in grams?

    A. 550 grams.
    B. 5500 grams
    C. 55 grams
    D. 55, 000grams

14. You are given the number 258, which of its factors are prime factors. You are required to mention all such values.

    i)1
    ii) 2
    iii) 3
    iv) 6
    v) 43

    A. 1,3,6
    B. 2, 3, 43
    C. 1. 43
    D. 2, 3, 43

15. Which of the following are not the prime numbers of factors of 456? You must mention all such numbers.

    A. 2
    B. 3
    C. 57
    D. 19

16. You have asked a student to write an expression that shows the quotient of a division operation is not always lesser than the dividend.

    A. 7÷5
    B. 11⅓ ÷1/4
    C. 80.5÷4.5
    D. 28÷7

17. You have asked a student to write an expression that shows the quotient of a division operation is not always lesser than the dividend.

    A. $27 \div 8$
    B. $10 \div 2$
    C. $7.15 \div 0.25$
    D. $5 \div 1/2$

18. The common theory states that the area of a square is greater than its perimeter. However, the rule is broken in one of the examples of sides of a square that are given below. Can you find out which one has a perimeter more than its area?

    A. a square with sides $\sqrt{36}$cms
    B. a square with sides 4.5cms
    C. a square with sides π
    D. a square with sides 8

19. Molly owns a grocery shop. She gives 2% off on all produce on Sundays. A carton of eggs in her shop costs $2.50 on all days except on Sunday. What would be the discounted price of a carton of eggs at her store on Sunday?

    A. $2.50
    B. $2.25
    C. $2
    D. $2.45

20. What is 423.8791 rounded off to its nearest hundredth?

    A. 423.88
    B. 423.86
    C. 423.888
    D. 423.900

21. What is 423.83321 rounded off to its nearest hundredth?

    A. 423.84
    B. 423.83

C. 423.8

D. 424

22. "The Sady's dryer" accepts only quarters as payments for the drying cycles of the clothes. Each quarter adds six minutes of dry time to the cycle. My jeans take one hour and a half to dry up completely. How many quarters do I need to ensure my jeans are fully dried?

A. 15

B. 9

C. 10

D. 12

23. In the sequence of numbers given below, each number is three more than two times the number preceding it. Find out the fourth number in the series.

4, 11, 25, —

A. 36

B. 54

C. 53

D. 46

24. Which one of the following numbers is a whole number?

A. 2

B. 2.2

C. 0.2

D. -2

25. Which one of the following is not a rational number?

A. -33

B. 3:5

C. √3

D. 1/3

26. Which of the following is not an integer?

    A. -5
    B. 5
    C. 5/7
    D. 0

27. **i)** Which of the following is a composite number?

    A. 16
    B. 3
    C. 19
    D. 13

    ii) Identify the "radical number."

    A. 64
    B. 4
    C. $\sqrt{27}$
    D. -8

28. What is the "place value" of 8 in the number 7685.234?

    A. hundreds
    B. tens
    C. hundredths
    D. tenths

29. A room is 12 feet long and 10 feet wide. What will be the approximate cost to carpet the room? Each yard of the carpet costs $14.50.

    A. $1500
    B. $580
    C. $750
    D. $1200

30. The perimeter of a rectangular house is 66 yards; its length is 33 feet. What is its width in yards?

    A. 18-yard
    B. 22-yard
    C. 32-yard
    D. 42-yard

31. The doctor has asked you to take 60 mg of a certain medication. The medication is in a liquid form, and 5ml of the liquid has 15mg of the dose. How many milliliters of the medicine do you need to take?

    A. 18ml
    B. 20ml
    C. 32ml
    D. 25ml

32. You need exactly 1840 cubic foot aquarium to keep the fish. The pet store you went to offers you four options, but they have length, width, and breadth measurements for the aquariums. Which aquarium will suit your purpose?

    A. 16 ft✕ 12 ft✕8 ft
    B. 23 ft✕10 ft✕8 ft
    C. 16 ft✕10 ft✕11ft
    D. 23 ft✕11ft✕8 ft

33. A matchbox is 0.15 feet long. Its length in inches would most closely be compared to which of the following articles?

    A. 1¼ inch paperclip
    B. 4 ⅕ inch lipstick
    C. 7 ⅔ inch crayon
    D. 6 ⅔ inch tube of a toothpaste

34. The diameter of a can is 6 inches, its height is 12 inches. What is the approximate volume of the can?

    A. 200 cubic inches
    B. 180.84 cubic inches
    C. 339 cubic inches
    D. 300 cubic inches

Answer Key

Reading

Q	A		Q	A
1	A		18	D
2	B		19	B
3	D		20	C
4	E		21	D
5	i) C ii) C		22	B
6	A		23	A
7	B		24	A
8	D		25	D
9	A		26	C
10	B		27	B
11	C		28	B
12	A		29	B
13	D		30	C
14	A		31	C
15	D		32	D
16	D		33	C
17	D		34	D

Writing

Q	A		Q	A
1	C		18	C
2	B		19	D
3	B		20	C
4	C		21	B
5	A		22	C
6	B		23	A
7	D		24	D
8	C		25	A
9	A		26	B
10	C		27	B
11	C		28	D
12	D		29	B
13	D		30	C
14	A		31	C
15	I) C II) C III) C IV) A		32	D
16	I) C II) C		33	D
17	i) A ii) B		34	D

Math

Q	1	2	3	4	5	6	7	8	9	10	11	12	13	14
A	B	C	A	D	C	C	C	C	B	C	D	D	B	D

Q	15	16	17	18	19	20	21	22	23	24	25	26	27
A	C	B	C	C	D	A	B	A	C	A	C	I) A II) C	D

Q	28	29	30	31	32	33	34
A	B	B	B	B	B	A	C

Answer Key and Explanations

Reading

1. **A**

    Only option A is valid; others do not apply to the text.

2. **B**

    Only option B can help us understand the observers' feelings or impressions of the knight at first sight.

3. **D**

    Fell is the past tense of "to fall;" Past and present are two different concepts; rain is a natural phenomenon that makes a kind of weather. Flush means having an even or leveled surface.

4. **E**

    Only cymbal has a c that is pronounced as s.

5. **i) C**

    The text mentions that Bea's parents were in the kitchen.

    ii) C

    The text is about Bea's Balloon Ride, undoubtedly this is the most important event.

6. **A**

    Comeback has two whole words, come and back. Backtalk is two separate words written as "a back talk."

7. **B**

   Pushback means negative or unfavorable response. In context to the text, option B is the most appropriate choice.

8. **D**

   horizontal.

   Supine means to lie flat with face upwards; its antonym is prone.

9. **A**

   penchant or inclination.

10. **B**

    The text never intended to scare one away from ODD. Parental frustration is also not the purpose for why the text was written. The text does not say that the parents are to be solely blamed for ODD.

11. **C**

    The text says there is no "single cure" for ODD, but does mention that ODD can be treated.

12. **A**

    Protagonist means the main figure of the story, or context.

13. **D**

    The author does not tell us about receiving immigrants without reservations or banning their entry. It doesn't tell us that immigrants destroy national integrity. Option D is something the text discusses.

14. **A**

The writer of the passage describes the theme of the book by showing a "direct example." The text does not mention that it is semi-autobiographical, although it mentions that the author draws inspiration from real-life events. The text does not suggest anywhere that you should read the book or what is the main idea of the novel.

15. **D**

the writer of the passage nowhere criticizes or encourages to gain the reader's interest. It also does not give any solid information about the novel. However, he probes deeper to *analyze* the text.

16. **D**

The text tells us that Chang-Rae's interest in writing novels came from his conflicting living status in America. It doesn't tell us whether others bullied him at school or if he entered essay competitions in school. His writing interest was not related to the Korean war.

17. **D**

The texts mention that all of Chang-Rae's characters are similar but do not mention that they are immigrants, males, or their knowledge of English speaking.

18. **D**

The author is concerned about the changing geopolitical conditions and cultural intermixing threatening the identity and security of the natives and the immigrants.

19. **B**

An incentive-based approach can be all of the options suggested, but in this context, B is best suited. Those who emit less will pay less.

20. **C**

The text does not give any know-how or suggest anything regarding the cause and effect of Greenhouse emissions. It does not suggest any conflicts between the two things.

21. **D**

D is the most appropriate choice and not C incentive-based approaches are *usually less costly* and may not be the "most effective" means.

22. **B**

Others are true, and C seems an enticing option, but the passage does not mention that incentive-based approaches are "smart choice." B is truc by default.

23. **A**

Cost-effective doesn't mean using resources or expending them without restrictions or doing things to impress. Things of the best quality may be costly, and cheaper products may give similar benefits. Option A gives the true explanation of the term.

24. **A**

Look at the tallest bar in the pictogram.

25. **D**

The bar diagram shows in 1960, recycling was near 10%.

26. **C**

Since we have no data before 1960, we do not know if the rate of recycling increased or decreased in 1960 compared to other times.

27. **B**

Recycling of glass declined in subsequent years.

28. **B**

The easiest way to use a dictionary is to alphabetize the words first and then look them up in order. To alphabetize, one must begin with the first letter of the word. If more than one word has the same first letter, consider the second letter, and so on. Alphabetizing is done on the letters of the word and not its length. Definitions should not be based solely on prior knowledge as one may not know the words or have a proper understanding of the definitions. The "synonym" function of the internet gives synonyms for that word; it may not provide a definition.

29. **B**

The knowledge of the vocabulary in a text is required; however, as the student is reading, they can understand the context of the text, and they must grasp the overall meaning. As a pre-reading strategy, you cannot make a list of unknown vocabulary words because you don't know what words are in the text unless you read them. The other options are effective prereading strategies. They help students engage with the text before starting to read it.

Suppose the text is a reading program where a list of more complex vocabulary words is present. In that case, the students can look up these words as part of the "prereading" process, but each reader needs to review different words.

Note: "Accessing" a text means to be able to gather information from it; in other words, to "get into" the text. Prereading strategies help to derive information even before a student has started reading.

As an examinee, you must be cautious about the following words in the questions: not, except, false, incorrect, least (likely), and such other negative word forms. These words change the meaning of your search for a correct answer.

30. **C**

The appropriate question to ask a student after reading the written directions for a task is "What do the directions mean?" You must instruct the student to paraphrase the directions in their words to ascertain their understanding. Asking "Do you understand?" or "Do those directions make sense?" results in an affirmative answer, not because the student understands the directions, but because saying no is embarrassing. "What questions do you have?" is an assumption that the student understands enough, which may not be true.

31. **C**

Asking why they did not bring more money or credit cards, or how did they feel when they found they could not enjoy their candy back home are irrelevant and even judgmental. The last question is best answered by asking what did they go to buy at the store.

32. **D**

Change in this context means cash.

33. **C**

Change means small denominations of money like pennies.

34. **D**

Reading slowly and loudly is of no benefit to the student and indeed, may make it more difficult for them to understand what is happening in the passage read. They may lose focus.

Writing

1. **C**

When we are using present-perfect "has never forgotten," a present tense "has an impressive memory" is the correct choice. Had (**A**) and did have (**B**) are past tense, while has had (**D**) is present-perfect tense. They all imply that he no longer has a remarkable memory, contradicting the sentence's meaning.

2. **B**

The scientists are still hoping for an action which is sometime in the future. The verb to find is most appropriate for this sentence. We could have used "of finding" instead of "to find."

3. **B**

The proper present-perfect tense of the transitive verb "to lay" is has laid. Has lain is intransitive. An example would be, "I have lain on this bed before." Have lain is a wrong use of verb tense and of using a plural form of an auxiliary verb with a singular subject. Is lying should be is laying, a present perfect continuous tense. But "is lying" would change the meaning of the sentence.

4. **C**

Using the past perfect tense "had bought" for the verb is correct because it is consistent with her action "consented to bring" something that she had done *before* she consented. Did buy is an awkward use of past tense bought and is inappropriate here.

The preposition should be at and not in. Prepositions are "function words" that indicate how a noun or a noun phrase is related to the rest of the sentence. Some like, in, on, after, since, imply temporal (related to time) or spatial (space) associations. In others, this association is more abstract, and the best choice for prepositions depends on the words around it. These prepositions are called "dependent prepositions." They do not follow precise rules.

Sometimes an odd preposition can change the meaning of the entire phrase of the sentence. For example, Danny ran into (and not in) the room with Roxy, the pet dog.

5. **A**

You should place a comma between a modifying clause or phrase and the clause it modifies. "That" is wrong usage (D), the adverb when was introduced at the beginning and should not be used again (B). Because is also incorrect for the same reason (C).

6. **B**

In this sentence, the predicate "did she know" is in the past tense. However, the fact remains true, and World Smile Day will always come on the first Friday in October. Hence, "comes on" is the right choice. Came on (A) denotes that it does not always happen, as do "has come on" (C) and had come on (D)

7. **D**

You should use present tense to describe something still existing. Also, since it is something to "see," sight will be more appropriate than site. Site means a location or spot.

8. **C**

Using "with" is the most precise use of a modifying prepositional phrase. "That has" is wordy and superfluous (A). Using the plural form of pronunciation with an apostrophe is wrong since it is not a possessive noun (A), and "have" is a plural form that disagrees with the singular subject in text (D).

9. **A**

The present tense of "to lie" is lies. "Lays," on the other hand, is the present tense of the transitive verb "to lay." A transitive verb takes its objects directly, for instance, "The warrior laid his sword on the ground." Has laid should be "has lain," the present perfect tense, but it is unsuitable since San Francisco is in the exact same location (d). Present progressive tense "is lying" is wrong for the same reason (b).

Lain is the present perfect or past perfect tense, and not a simple present tense, and it also lacks the accompanying auxiliary has or had (c).

10. **C**

The most appropriate choice here is the simple past tense sank. Sunk in American usage is part of present perfect "has sunk," "is sunk," or "has been sunk" (passive voice), and past perfect "had sunk," "was sunk," or "had been sunk" (passive voice). We use the past perfect tense to link events in the past to a later time, usually the present. Hence use of past participle is unwarranted in this sentence.

11. **C**

"Any" can be used to suggest a singular or plural number. In this context, the choice of a plural form is more appropriate. When asking questions with plural count nouns, use any in the plural sense. Thus it should be "has any one of the relatives? (d)" "Are any of the" is incorrect because we have used "been ushered" (past perfect) in the sentence (b).

12. **D**

The choice of the preposition "in" is wrong for this sentence. "For" is a more appropriate and commonly used term.

Neither is singular; hence, you should use the verb form expects. Expect goes with a plural number (A). "has expected" is present perfect and not valid (c). "Is expecting" is present progressive and is wrong in this context. It would have been appropriate to use is expecting if the sentence allowed for "until now." The present progressive denotes a current action, an action in progress, or an unfinished action.

13. **D**

"Had sold out" in active voice is improper because the tickets cannot sell out by themselves (A). The use of passive voice is more appropriate for this sentence. Rather than a simple past tense like were sold out (in the passive voice) (c), "had been sold out" is better as the action of selling out preceded the movie in town. "For" is a wrong choice of a preposition, and the word should have been far.

14. **A**

The choice of verb form in singular or plural number for this sentence depends on the subject, The Origins, which is in plural form. Hence even if existence, a collective noun is in the singular form, the correct use of the verb should take a plural form. Choice of existences in this context is inappropriate B, and C. D is incorrect because the singular form of the verb used "has been." The present perfect tense makes sense when a time frame for the action is mentioned c). Hence, answer A is the best choice.

15. **i) C**

Of all the options given in the answers, reserve is the only noun. Its use implies a source of protected resources.

ii) C

Cartilage is the noun. True is an adjective qualifying the noun fish; Their is a possessive pronoun, and not is used as a determiner in this sentence to indicate the opposite of what is specified.

iii) C

"Words" is a noun, backward is an adjective, and Sheila is a proper noun. Note, "used to" can also be used as an adjective; for instance, "Sheila used to recite words backward." In this sentence used to means Sheila is habituated to the task. Similarly, if we say Sheila is used to tea, we use "used to" as an adjective since it means that Sheila is addicted to tea.

iv) A

Infiltrate is the verb; it means to gain access surreptitiously.

16. **i) C**

Wet is an adjective, papers is a noun, in is a preposition. Laid is the past participle of the verb form "to lay," and "were" is the auxiliary verb.

ii) C

Receive is the verb. Decision and destruction are nouns, and rash is an adjective qualifying the noun decision.

17. **i) A**

Since Sam said something, it should be within quotes; hence d) is wrong. Doberman should be capitalized; dog and pinscher are not capitalized. The part of the breed that comes from a proper noun is capitalized, whereas the part from a common noun is not. Hence, "German shepherd" should have a capital "G" for German but a lowercase "s" for shepherd. The rules are similar in French bulldog and English foxhound, and we use lowercase for a cocker spaniel or golden retriever. The use of the preposition "about" is redundant but not wrong.

ii) B

Eclectic means broad and diverse range of tastes. It also means having refined and exquisite tastes.

18. **C**

It should be it's and not its.

19. **D**

A comma or a semicolon is unnecessary and incorrect between a noun and its proper name, in this case, work and self-reliance. The best choice for the preposition in this context should be about and not of.

20. **C**

There should be no punctuation between the verb and its object. This is also true when the object is a title within quotation marks, as is the case here. Therefore, the dash, comma, and colon are all incorrect.

21. **B**

In December is the future. Hence, the use of the future tense auxiliary verb "will" is appropriate use. Will have married cannot be for a period of ten years as being married is a continuous process. Will be married suggests we are not yet married. Adding will to have been makes the tense future perfect and appropriate for the sentence. Thirty-five should be hyphenated.

22. **C**

Since the book is still read and existing, usage of the present tense is preferable to past tense. In choice d), the apostrophe has been erroneously omitted. A simple present tense is preferable to present perfect in this context.

23. **A**

Subject names of languages like English, French, etc., are always capitalized. Names of subjects other than this are common names and hence, not capitalized. Names of courses like Algebra and Geometry, however, must be capitalized. We do not use semicolons to separate phrases in a series. Semicolons can introduce lists or explanations and separate only independent clauses or phrases having internal commas.

24. **D**

You need not capitalize arts. What turns you on is slang and should never be used in texts. Which you choose is preferable to what you select. Using "which" is more appropriate when you choose something from a list.

25. **A**

Usage of italicized words for the Greek derivatives is correct and you should use a comma after each such word. The inside quotation marks surrounding the English translation are correct. Separating these items with a dash is wrong. A dash followed by a comma is incorrect, and so is the use of a hyphen to separate a pair. Both pairs should be separated by a comma.

26. **B**

Jellyfish is a single word; using the plural jellyfishes is unnecessary. You can use one jellyfish. Seeing does not correspond with make.

Each of the animals on display should be separated by a comma; however, a comma before and is redundant.

Omitting the comma in d) before is wrong. The killer whale is not a proper name and need not be capitalized unless the sentence starts with it. Jellyfish is a single word. Using two words for it is wrong.

27. **B**

In d) there is a disagreement of verb, it cannot be other solar system "is"there. In c), "maybe" clashes with "fact," and in A, there is no comma between an independent clause and the subsequent phrase.

28. **D**

A semicolon separates two independent clauses. A comma cannot be the correct substitute A. Time-saving should be hyphenated. Hence B and c) are wrong choices. Further, using a second semicolon to offset the latter underlined section is incorrect. d) is right because time-saving is hyphenated and correct; using a semicolon to separate two independent clauses is also the right choice.

Using "should" and "could" instead of "can" changes the implication of the sentence.

29. **B**

The tense should be past tense, "made".

30. **C**

Stacy and Clara should be plural, "are going". They don't like sports, but both are going to the movie instead.

31. **C**

Audience is singular and hence, use "applauds" as verb form.

32. **D**

London cannot surely lie beneath us. The sentence can be rewritten as, "After we descended through the clouds, London lay beneath us."

33. **D**

There is the use of the wrong subject-verb agreement. The valet **brings** in the car. The owners of the car **are** happy. Cars travel faster on Expressways than on most other **roads.** Which of the following sentences **does** not use the apostrophe correctly?

Dangling modifiers describe something that is not there in the sentence; a squinting modifier describes two likely items in a sentence but fails to identify which one it is modifying.

34. **D**

It refers to the painting, and hence, it is a pronoun. Rose is the only noun in the sentence. It can also be used as a noun, for example, "This is it."

Math

1. **B**

If you go through the tables "a" and "b" separately, you will notice that in both the tables, the numbers have increased in subsequent rows. While in table "a," the value of numbers has increased by 1, in table "b," the values have increased by 1.5.

Therefore, the table can be written as,

a	b
1	1.5
2 (1+1)	3 (1.5+1.5)
3 (2+1)	4.5 (3+1.5)
4 (3+1)	6 (4.5+1.5)
5	7.5
6	9

2. **C**

The catering company uses 5 pineapples to make the special fruit salad. They use the same number of mangoes as pineapples. Therefore, 5 mangoes go into the salad. The number of apples should be **25** because they use 5 apples for each mango, and the number of mangoes used is 5.

They also used pears, three per apple. 25 apples= 25*3=75 pears.

Therefore Bobby's catering company uses 5 pineapples+ 5 mangoes+ 25 apples+ 75 pears=110 fruits are used in their most recent batch of fruit salad.

3. **A**

20 liters of aquarium water has 4 tablespoons of salt.

1 liter of the same aquarium water has 4/20 tablespoons of salt.

50 liters of the same aquarium water has (4/20)*50 tablespoons of salt.

Or, 50 liters of the same aquarium water has 50/5 tablespoons of salt

or, The 50 liters aquarium has 10 tablespoons of salt.

But, Jill already had added 4 tablespoons of salt. So, she needs to put 6 tablespoons of salt into the water to maintain the same salinity as before.

Another way to do the sum is to determine how much water Jill must add to make a 50 liters aquarium from the previous 20-liter capacity. 50-20=30

If Jill adds 4 tablespoons of salt to 20 liters of water, then she will have to add 20/4*30=6 tablespoons of salt.

4. **D**

In 20 minutes, the number of nuggets hauled into a box is 25.

The workers can haul 25/20 nuggets into a box in 1 minute.

The number of nuggets collected in the box after 2 hours, or 120 minutes will be (25/20)*120

Or, 150 nuggets.

5. **C**

Let us find out what each of the shares means for Bob.

⅕ of ½ =1/10th of the share of profits.

⅗ of ⅔ =⅖th of the profit's share.

⅘ of ¾ =⅗th of the profit's share.

⅘ of ¼ =⅕th of the profit's share.

If we arrange the fractions serially, we may write 1/10, ⊠, ⊠, ⊠.

The easiest way to compare the fractions is to convert their denominators to a single value. The least common denominator for all these fractions is 10. Since the denominator of the first fraction is already 10, we do not need to change it. For the rest of the fractions, multiplying the numerator and the denominator by 2 will give us 4/10, 6/10, and 2/10, respectively.

The values can now be written as

1/10. 4/10, 6/10, and 2/10.

Clearly, Bobby will benefit if he chooses the third option for sharing their profits.

6. **C**

Bob will earn 6/10-4/10 =2/10 or 1/5th more if he chooses option C.

7. **C**

The fractions are ⅙,⅛, 2/10 or ⅕

The least common denominator is the smallest number that can be a common denominator for a set of fractions. It is the lowest number you can use in the denominator to create a set of equivalent fractions with the same denominator.

Or, 2*2*2*3*5=120

To convert the fractions, you may write,

⅙= ⅙ *20/20 =20/120

⅛ = ⅛ * 15/15=15/120

2/10= 2/10*12/12=24/120

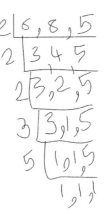

8. **C**

4a+27+b5=c14

First, let us consider the unit's column.

a+7+5=14

a=14-12

Or, a=2.

Now we can write the equation as

42+27+b5=c**14**

For the ten's column; we have to carry 1 from the unit's column.

1+4+2+b=11

b=11–7

Or, b=4.

Since we have the values for a and b, we can write the left-hand side of the equation as

42+27+45=c14

If you add 42+27+45, you get **114**.

The value of c is, therefore, 1.

a=2, b=4, and c=1

9. **B**

The first step of the sum is addition. You are to add –3 from a bigger number 5. When you add a positive and a negative number, use the sign of the larger number and divide the smaller from it. 5–3=2.

In the second step, you are to subtract the negative number –5 from 2. You can write this as

2–(–5)

Or, 2+5

Or, 7

10. **C**

1.5+6.44+19+25.52+42.55= 95.01=95 is the nearest tenth value. The difference from the exact sum 95.01 is 0.01

11. **D**

149,750 can be rounded to 150,000. 90, 190 on the other hand, can be rounded to 90,200. The difference between the two rounded-up numbers is 60,000 - 200 or 59,800. While the first rounded-up number is more than the original by 250, the latter is more than the original number by 10. Their sum is 250. You can mentally take out 250 from 59,800. You will get 59,550, or approximately 59,600.

12. **D**

The sum now stands 95.05, which when rounded up to the nearest tenth value is 95.1. The whole number is 95. If you subtract 95 from 95.1, you get 0 .05. Therefore, answer D is correct.

13. **B**

The answer is 5500 grams. 1 kilogram= 1000grams. Therefore, 5.5 kilograms = 5500 grams.

14. **D**

Although 258 seems a complicated number to find its factors without being able to calculate it, fortunately, the teacher did the calculation for us. They mentioned numbers 1, 2, 3, 6, and 43; our task is to determine which of these factors are prime numbers.

We know that prime numbers are whole numbers that are greater than 1. Therefore, 1 is not a prime number. The priming number has factors 1 and itself. While 2, 3, and 43 fit into the definition of prime number, 6 does not.

15. **C**

Only 57 is divisible by factors 1, 3, and itself. The rest are divisible only by 1 and itself, making them prime numbers.

16. **B**

This can only happen when the divisor is significantly less than the dividend. In case of example B 11⅓ or, 34/3 ÷ 1/4 = 34*4/3 = 45.66. Usually, this is not the rule. We know that dividend ÷ divisor = quotient. Therefore, the quotient should be smaller than the dividend.

11⅓ is an improper fraction, which can be written as 34/3. Since you are dividing it with ¼, you can write the equation as 34/3 ÷ 1/4 = 34/3*4= 136/3.

17. **C**

The steps of decimal division are first, you have to set up the division.

7.15 ÷ 0.25

In the second step, you have to move the decimal points until the divisor is an integer.

When you shift the decimal points of both sides by the same degree to get the integer 25 as the divisor, you get 715 ÷ 25.

Or, 28 is the quotient which is significantly more than 7.15

We may say that a quotient can be more than the dividend when the divisors are fractions or decimals.

18. **C**

A square is a geometric figure with all its sides equal. Its perimeter is the sum of all its sides. The area of the square is side². In all instances, the perimeter as the "sum" is less than the area of the squares, which is side*side. The only exception is ⊠, or 22/7

The area of a square is smaller than its perimeter if its sides are less than four. When its sides are four, then the area of the square is the same as its perimeter.

19. **D**

   2% of $2.50 is 2*2.50/100

   Or, 5/100

   or, $0.05

   Now, we must subtract 0.05 from 2.50.

   The answer is $2.45

20. **A**

   The first position after a decimal is the tenth position, and the next is the hundredth position after a decimal.

21. **B**

   C is incorrect because 423.8 is not the same as 423.83. Since the third digit after the decimal point is a recurring 3, you can safely round off the number as 423.83. However, the situation would have changed if the third digit after the decimal was more than five. You should then choose 4 instead of 3 as the digit in the hundredth position after the decimal. Refer to question **#20** to follow.

22. **A**

   One and half hours when converted to minutes is 90 minutes. Each drying cycle lasts for six minutes. Therefore 90 minutes has 15 cycles of drying. Since a quarter is needed to run a cycle, I will need 15 quarters to dry my jeans completely.

23. **C**

   The number preceding the missing number is 25. The missing number is two times and three more than this number. Two times 25 is 50. Add three to get 53.

24. **A**

   The whole numbers are all positive integers, including zero. The whole number cannot have any decimal or fractional part. A whole number cannot be negative.

25. **C**

   Irrational numbers are numbers that cannot be represented by simple fractions or in the form of a ratio. They have an endless number of non-repetitive digits after the decimal point. -33, a negative number can be expressed as the quotient of two integers 33 and 1, and hence is a rational number (but not a whole number). Irrational numbers cannot be expressed as simple ratios between two integers, and 3:5 is not irrational. ⅓ forms a repeating decimal 3.6666, and is not irrational.

   $\sqrt{3}$ is irrational, it cannot be further simplified, and the numbers after the decimal points (1.732) are nonterminating and non-repetitive.

26. **C**

   Integers are whole numbers, positive, negative, and zero. They are not fractions or decimals.

27. **i) A**

   Composite numbers are those numbers that are greater than 1 and have more than 2 factors (1 and itself). 16 has more than two factors, the rest are more than one, but none has more than two factors.

   ii) C

   Radical numbers are the square roots.

28. **B**

   The positions of the numbers are as follows: 7= thousands, 6= hundreds, 8= tens, and 5= ones. After the decimal, the place values of the integers are 2=tenths, 3= hundredths, and 4= thousandths.

29. **B**

The area of a room is the product of its length and width or 120feet. But, we have to convert it to the yard because the carpet is measured in yards. Conversion is easy. To convert a yard into a foot, multiply with 3. Divide with 3 to convert from the foot into the yard.

Therefore, 120 feet is= 120/3=40
The cost of carpet is $14.50 /yard.
Therefore the cost of carpeting the room is 40*14.50=$580

30. **B**

The perimeter of a rectangle is 2L+2W, where L=length, and W=Width.

Therefore, we can write the equation as 2L +2W=Perimeter

The perimeter of the house is given in yards, and its length is in feet. They must be converted into the same unit. Since the answer is in the yard, we will convert the length of the house in the yard.

2*11+2W=66

Or, 22+2W=66,

Or, 2W=44

Or, W=22 yards.

31. **B**

This is an example from proportion. The equation can be written as the following.

5/15 = x/60

3 ~~15~~x = 60*~~5~~

x= 20ml

32. **B**

    You need to do a little back-calculation here. None of the other values, when multiplied, give an exact 1840 cubic feet. But 23 ft×10 ft×8 ft = 1840 cubic feet.

33. **A**

    1 feet=12 inches.

    Therefore 0.15 feet =12×0.15 =1.80 inches.

    Now you need to convert it into a fraction.

    1.80=180/100

    Or, 9/5

    It is a mixed fraction corresponding to 1⅘ inch, which is approximately the size of the paperclip mentioned in the sum.

34. **C**

    A can is an example of a cylinder. The volume of a cylinder is expressed as $\pi r^2 h$, where r=radius and h=height.

    In the sum given to you, the diameter of the can is 6 inches. Therefore r =3, and r^2 =9 inches. h=12 inches.

    The volume is, therefore, π×9×12

    We know π=3.14

    Our answer is 3.14×108

    Or, 339.12 cubic inches, approx. 339 cubic inches.

Conclusion

The ETS-Praxis test is a computer-based test to check the general proficiency of the examinee. It has three parts, each 85 minutes in duration. There are 56 selected-response questions from each category, reading, writing, and mathematics. The reading section tests the examinee's capability to draw logical inferences from the texts or visuals, structure and language skills, and integration of knowledge and ideas.

The reading test contains paired passages totaling approximately 200 words, and four to seven questions are based on it. There are long passages of approximately 200 words with four to seven questions, short passages of approximately 100 words with two or three questions, and short sentences followed by a single question. Passages are taken from both print and electronic media and visuals like diagrams, charts, drawings, maps, floor plans, or graphs.

The test may also contain questions that will not be scored.

Look for words like not, except, false, incorrect, least, likely, and any negative word forms in questions. These words will change the purpose of the search for the correct answer.

Words like better, best, most, main, major, and primary or primarily in questions indicate that there might be other workable answers, but the correct answer is the one that is the best choice.

The math section consists of 30 multiple choice questions based on number sense, basic algebra, geometry, measurement, and data analysis.

This book has gone through all the sections in great detail, keeping in mind the type of questions that are asked in the examination. While the first section has extensively dealt with theory, the second part of the book is totally dedicated to practical parts, with 34 questions from each of the segments in three different modules. You can even try a timed test to see if you can finish the test under exam conditions. Questions have been given from all the relevant topics and are widely distributed in their variety. Taking the tests will certainly alleviate examination fear.

References

Aarts, B. (2011). *Oxford Modern English Grammar.* Oxford.

Barrett, Grant; (2016). *Perfect English Grammar: The Indispensable Guide to Excellent Writing and Speaking.* Zephyros Pr.

Nazari, Reza:. (2022). *ParaPro Math Workbook: A Comprehensive Review + 2 Full Length ParaPro Math Practice Tests .*

Test Prep for the ParaPro Assessment. (2022). Https://Www.Ets.Org/Parapro/Test_prep/ Materials.

Triscell, H. (2018). *Paraprofessional Study Guide - Paraprofessional Audio Study Guide - Parapro Study Guide: READING EDITION - BEST Paraprofessional Test Prep - Be READY For The Paraprofessional Test!!*

Verma, R. (2018). *Fast Track Objective Arithmetic .* Arihant.

Wynne, S. A. (2010). *Praxis Parapro Assessment 0755: Teacher Certification Exam: 1 (XAM PRAXIS).* Xamonline.

Made in the USA
Las Vegas, NV
03 October 2022